# Contents

# MOM'S BEST MACARONI SALAD

**Servings: 16 | Prep: 30m | Cooks: 0m | Total: 30m**

## NUTRITION FACTS

Calories: 424 | Carbohydrates: 45g | Fat: 24.7g | Protein: 6.6g | Cholesterol: 19mg

## INGREDIENTS

- 16 ounces uncooked elbow macaroni
- 2 cups mayonnaise
- 4 carrots, shredded
- 1 (14 ounce) can sweetened condensed milk
- 1 large red onion, chopped
- 1/2 cup white sugar
- 1/2 green bell pepper, seeded and chopped
- 1/2 cup white vinegar
- 1/2 red bell pepper, seeded and chopped
- salt and pepper to taste
- 1 cup chopped celery

## DIRECTIONS

1. Bring a large pot of lightly salted water to a boil. Add macaroni, and cook until tender, about 8 minutes. Rinse under cold water, and drain.
2. In a large bowl, stir together the carrots, red onion, green pepper, red pepper and celery. Mix in the mayonnaise, condensed milk, sugar, vinegar, salt and pepper. Add the macaroni, toss gently, cover and refrigerate for at least 8 hours. I usually make this a day ahead of time, and stir it occasionally to blend the flavors. The macaroni will absorb some of the liquid.

# GREEK ORZO SALAD

**Servings: 6 | Prep: 1h10m | Cooks: 10m | Total: 1h20m**

## NUTRITION FACTS

Calories: 326 | Carbohydrates: 48.7g | Fat: 10.2g | Protein: 13.1g | Cholesterol: 22mg

## INGREDIENTS

- 1 1/2 cups uncooked orzo pasta
- 1 (2 ounce) can black olives, drained
- 2 (6 ounce) cans marinated artichoke hearts
- 1/4 cup chopped fresh parsley
- 1 tomato, seeded and chopped

- 1 tablespoon lemon juice
- 1 cucumber, seeded and chopped
- 1/2 teaspoon dried oregano
- 1 red onion, chopped
- 1/2 teaspoon lemon pepper
- 1 cup crumbled feta cheese

## DIRECTIONS

1. Bring a large pot of lightly salted water to a boil. Add pasta and cook for 8 to 10 minutes or until al dente; drain. Drain artichoke hearts, reserving liquid.
2. In large bowl combine pasta, artichoke hearts, tomato, cucumber, onion, feta, olives, parsley, lemon juice, oregano and lemon pepper. Toss and chill for 1 hour in refrigerator.
3. Just before serving, drizzle reserved artichoke marinade over salad.

# BLT PASTA SALAD

**Servings: 10 | Prep: 15m | Cooks: 10m | Total: 3h25m | Additional: 3h**

## NUTRITION FACTS

Calories: 341 | Carbohydrates: 38.2g | Fat: 15.5g | Protein: 12.2g | Cholesterol: 26mg

## INGREDIENTS

- 1 (16 ounce) package medium seashell pasta
- 1 small onion, chopped
- 1 pound sliced bacon
- 2 tomatoes, chopped
- 1 1/2 cups light Ranch-style salad dressing

## DIRECTIONS

1. Bring a large pot of lightly salted water to a boil. Add the pasta, and cook until tender, about 8 minutes. Drain, and rinse under cold water to cool.
2. Meanwhile, cook the bacon in a large deep skillet over medium-high heat until browned and crisp. Remove from the pan and drain on paper towels.
3. In a large bowl, stir together the Ranch dressing, onion, and tomatoes. Mix in the cooled pasta. The pasta will absorb some of the dressing, so don't worry if it seems like too much. Refrigerate for several hours or overnight. Crumble bacon over the top just before serving.

# GARDEN PASTA SALAD

**Servings: 10 | Prep: 15m | Cooks: 15m | Total: 1h30m**

## NUTRITION FACTS

Calories: 449 | Carbohydrates: 45.1g | Fat: 27.4g | Protein: 8.4g | Cholesterol: 4mg

## INGREDIENTS

- 1 (16 ounce) package uncooked tri-color spiral pasta
- 2 large tomatoes, diced
- 1/2 cup thinly sliced carrots
- 1/4 cup chopped onion
- 2 stalks celery, chopped
- 2 (16 ounce) bottles Italian-style salad dressing
- 1/2 cup chopped green bell pepper
- 1/2 cup grated Parmesan cheese
- 1/2 cup cucumber, peeled and thinly sliced

## DIRECTIONS

1. Cook pasta in large pot of boiling water until al dente. Rinse under cold water, and drain.
2. Mix chopped carrots, celery, cucumber, green pepper, tomatoes, and onion together in large bowl.
3. Combine cooled pasta and vegetables together in large bowl. Pour Italian dressing over mixture, add Parmesan cheese and mix well.
4. Chill for one hour before serving.

# SPINACH AND TORTELLINI SALAD

**Servings: 4 | Prep: 15m | Cooks: 15m | Total: 30m**

## NUTRITION FACTS

Calories: 377 | Carbohydrates: 33.1g | Fat: 23.2g | Protein: 13.1g | Cholesterol: 17mg

## INGREDIENTS

- 1 (9 ounce) package cheese-filled tortellini
- 2 cups cherry tomatoes, halved
- 1 (10 ounce) package frozen chopped spinach, thawed and drained
- 1 (2 ounce) can sliced black olives
- 1/3 cup grated Parmesan cheese
- 1 (8 ounce) bottle Italian-style salad dressing

## DIRECTIONS

1. In a large pot of salted boiling water, cook pasta until al dente, rinse under cold water and drain.
2. In a large bowl, combine the tortellini, spinach, cheese, tomatoes and olives. Add enough salad dressing to coat. Toss and season with salt and pepper.

# ASIAN SALAD
**Servings: 10 | Prep: 20m | Cooks: 10m | Total: 30m**

## NUTRITION FACTS

Calories: 374 | Carbohydrates: 19.5g | Fat: 32.3g | Protein: 4.7g | Cholesterol: 24mg

## INGREDIENTS

- 2 (3 ounce) packages ramen noodles, crushed
- 1 bunch green onions, chopped
- 1 cup blanched slivered almonds
- 3/4 cup vegetable oil
- 2 teaspoons sesame seeds
- 1/4 cup distilled white vinegar
- 1/2 cup butter, melted
- 1/2 cup white sugar
- 1 head napa cabbage, shredded
- 2 tablespoons soy sauce

## DIRECTIONS

1. In a medium skillet over low heat brown ramen noodles, almonds, and sesame seeds with melted butter or margarine. Once browned, take off heat and cool.
2. In a small saucepan bring vegetable oil, sugar, and vinegar to boil for 1 minute. Cool. Add soy sauce.
3. In a large bowl, combine shredded napa cabbage and chopped green onions. Add the noodle and soy sauce mixture. Toss to coat. Serve.

# GREEK PASTA SALAD
**Servings: 8 | Prep: 20m | Cooks: 10m | Total: 3h30m**

## NUTRITION FACTS

Calories: 307 | Carbohydrates: 19.3g | Fat: 23.6g | Protein: 5.4g | Cholesterol: 14mg

## INGREDIENTS

- 2 cups penne pasta
- 10 cherry tomatoes, halved
- 1/4 cup red wine vinegar
- 1 small red onion, chopped
- 1 tablespoon lemon juice
- 1 green bell pepper, chopped

- 2 cloves garlic, crushed
- 1 red bell pepper, chopped
- 2 teaspoons dried oregano
- 1/2 cucumber, sliced
- salt and pepper to taste
- 1/2 cup sliced black olives
- 2/3 cup extra-virgin olive oil
- 1/2 cup crumbled feta cheese

## DIRECTIONS

1. Fill a large pot with lightly salted water and bring to a rolling boil over high heat. Once the water is boiling, stir in the penne, and return to a boil. Cook the pasta uncovered, stirring occasionally, until the pasta has cooked through, but is still firm to the bite, about 11 minutes. Rinse with cold water and drain well in a colander set in the sink.
2. Whisk together the vinegar, lemon juice, garlic, oregano, salt, pepper, and olive oil. Set aside. Combine pasta, tomatoes, onion, green and red peppers, cucumber, olives, and feta cheese in a large bowl. Pour vinaigrette over the pasta and mix together. Cover and chill for 3 hours before serving.

# MANDARIN CHICKEN PASTA SALAD

**Servings: 6 | Prep: 45m | Cooks: 8m | Total: 53m**

## NUTRITION FACTS

Calories: 425 | Carbohydrates: 44.7g | Fat: 18.9g | Protein: 21.8g | Cholesterol: 35mg

## INGREDIENTS

- 1 teaspoon finely chopped, peeled fresh ginger
- 1/2 cup diced red bell pepper
- 1/3 cup rice vinegar
- 1/2 cup coarsely chopped red onion
- 1/4 cup orange juice
- 2 diced Roma tomatoes
- 1/4 cup vegetable oil
- 1 carrot, shredded
- 1 teaspoon toasted sesame oil
- 1 (6 ounce) bag fresh spinach
- 1 (1 ounce) package dry onion soup mix
- 1 (11 ounce) can mandarin orange segments, drained
- 2 teaspoons white sugar
- 2 cups diced cooked chicken
- 1 clove garlic, pressed

- 1/2 cup sliced almonds, toasted
- 1 (8 ounce) package bow tie (farfalle) pasta
- 1/2 cucumber - scored, halved lengthwise, seeded, and sliced

## DIRECTIONS

1. To make the dressing, whisk together the ginger root, rice vinegar, orange juice, vegetable oil, sesame oil, soup mix, sugar, and garlic until well blended. Cover, and refrigerate until needed.
2. Bring a large pot of lightly salted water to a boil. Add the bowtie pasta and cook for 8 to 10 minutes or until al dente; drain, and rinse under cold water. Place pasta in a large bowl.
3. To make the salad, toss the cucumber, bell pepper, onion, tomatoes, carrot, spinach, mandarin oranges, chicken, and almonds with the pasta. Pour the dressing over the salad mixture, and toss again to coat evenly. Serve immediately.

# SPINACH PASTA SALAD

**Servings: 8 | Prep: 10m | Cooks: 15m | Total: 2h25m**

## NUTRITION FACTS

Calories: 334 | Carbohydrates: 41.8g | Fat: 16.6g | Protein: 8.6g | Cholesterol: 6mg

## INGREDIENTS

- 1 (12 ounce) package farfalle pasta
- 1 cup Italian-style salad dressing
- 10 ounces baby spinach, rinsed and torn into bite-size piece
- 4 cloves garlic, minced
- 2 ounces crumbled feta cheese with basil and tomato
- 1 lemon, juiced
- 1 red onion, chopped
- 1/2 teaspoon garlic salt
- 1 (15 ounce) can black olives, drained and chopped
- 1/2 teaspoon ground black pepper

## DIRECTIONS

1. In a large pot of salted boiling water, cook pasta until al dente, rinse under cold water and drain.
2. In a large bowl, combine the pasta, spinach, cheese, red onion and olives.
3. Whisk together the salad dressing, garlic, lemon juice, garlic salt and pepper. Pour over salad and toss. Refrigerate for 2 hours and serve chilled.

# CHICKEN CLUB PASTA SALAD

**Servings: 6 | Prep: 20m | Cooks: 10m | Total: 30m**

## NUTRITION FACTS

Calories: 485 | Carbohydrates: 37.1g | Fat: 30.1g | Protein: 19.2g | Cholesterol: 48mg

## INGREDIENTS

- 8 ounces corkscrew-shaped pasta
- 1 cup cubed Muenster cheese
- 3/4 cup Italian-style salad dressing
- 1 cup chopped celery
- 1/4 cup mayonnaise
- 1 cup chopped green bell pepper
- 2 cups chopped, cooked rotisserie chicken
- 8 ounces cherry tomatoes, halved
- 12 slices crispy cooked bacon, crumbled
- 1 avocado - peeled, pitted, and chopped

## DIRECTIONS

1. Bring a large pot of lightly salted water to a boil. Cook pasta in the boiling water, stirring occasionally until cooked through but firm to the bite, 10 to 12 minutes. Drain and rinse under cold water.
2. Whisk Italian-style dressing and mayonnaise together in a large bowl. Stir pasta, chicken, bacon, Muenster cheese, celery, green bell pepper, cherry tomatoes, and avocado into dressing until evenly coated.

# CLASSIC MACARONI SALAD
### Servings: 12 | Prep: 20m | Cooks: 8m | Total: 4h33m

## NUTRITION FACTS

Calories: 295 | Carbohydrates: 32g | Fat: 16.1g | Protein: 5.4g | Cholesterol: 7mg

## INGREDIENTS

- 1 cup mayonnaise
- 3/4 cup diced red bell pepper
- 1/4 cup white vinegar
- 1/2 cup grated carrot
- 2 tablespoons Dijon mustard
- 1/2 cup chopped green onions, white and light parts
- 2 teaspoons kosher salt, or more to taste
- 1/4 cup diced jalapeno pepper
- 1/2 teaspoon ground black pepper

- 1/4 cup diced poblano pepper
- 1/8 teaspoon cayenne pepper
- 1 (16 ounce) package uncooked elbow macaroni
- 1 tablespoon white sugar, or more to taste
- 1 tablespoon mayonnaise (optional)
- 1 cup finely diced celery
- 1 tablespoon water (optional)

## DIRECTIONS

1. Whisk 1 cup mayonnaise, vinegar, Dijon mustard, salt, black pepper, and cayenne pepper together in a bowl until well blended; whisk in sugar. Stir in celery, red bell pepper, carrot, onions, and jalapeno and poblano peppers. Refrigerate until macaroni is ready to dress.
2. Bring a large pot of well salted water to a boil. Cook elbow macaroni in the boiling water, stirring occasionally until cooked through, 8 to 10 minutes. Drain but do not rinse. Allow macaroni to drain in a colander about 5 minutes, shaking out moisture from time to time. Pour macaroni into large bowl; toss to separate and cool to room temperature. Macaroni should be sticky.
3. Pour dressing over macaroni and stir until dressing is evenly distributed. Cover with plastic wrap. Refrigerate at least 4 hours or, ideally, overnight to allow dressing to absorb into the macaroni.
4. Stir salad before serving. Mix 1 tablespoon mayonnaise and 1 tablespoon water into salad for fresher look.

# ITALIAN PASTA SALAD
### Servings: 12 | Prep: 15m | Cooks: 15m | Total: 30m

## NUTRITION FACTS

Calories: 291 | Carbohydrates: 32.6g | Fat: 14.6g | Protein: 8.5g | Cholesterol: 6mg

## INGREDIENTS

- 1 (16 ounce) package rotini pasta
- 1 red bell pepper, diced
- 1 cup Italian-style salad dressing
- 1 green bell pepper, chopped
- 1 cup creamy Caesar salad dressing
- 1 red onion, diced
- 1 cup grated Parmesan cheese

## DIRECTIONS

1. In a large pot of salted boiling water, cook pasta until al dente, rinse under cold water and drain.
2. In a large bowl, combine the pasta, Italian salad dressing, Caesar dressing, Parmesan cheese, red bell pepper, green bell pepper, and red onion. Mix well and serve chilled or at room temperature.

# AWESOME HAM PASTA SALAD
## Servings: 6 | Prep: 15m | Cooks: 12m | Total: 27m

## NUTRITION FACTS

Calories: 697 | Carbohydrates: 44.9g | Fat: 48.2g | Protein: 21.3g | Cholesterol: 65mg

## INGREDIENTS

- 8 ounces ziti pasta
- 1 cup mayonnaise
- 1 pound cooked ham, cubed
- 1/2 cup sour cream
- 1 large red bell pepper, cut into 1 inch pieces
- 2 1/2 teaspoons beef bouillon granules
- 1 large green bell pepper, cut into 1 inch pieces
- 1 tablespoon white vinegar
- 1 large red onion, coarsely chopped
- 1/2 teaspoon salt
- 15 small sweet pickles, chopped, juice reserved
- 1/4 teaspoon ground black pepper
- 1 cup cherry tomatoes, halved
- 2 cloves garlic, minced

## DIRECTIONS

1. Bring a large pot of lightly salted water to a boil. Add pasta and cook for 8 to 10 minutes or until al dente; drain.
2. In a large bowl, mix together the drained pasta, ham, peppers, onion, pickles and tomatoes.
3. In a small bowl, whisk together the mayonnaise, sour cream, beef bouillon granules, vinegar, salt, pepper, garlic and 1/2 cup of reserved pickle juice. Fold into the salad and toss gently until evenly coated. Chill overnight to allow the flavors to blend. Serve near room temperature.

# SUN-DRIED TOMATO BASIL ORZO
## Servings: 8 | Prep: 15m | Cooks: 8m | Total: 23m

## NUTRITION FACTS

Calories: 255 | Carbohydrates: 38.8g | Fat: 6.9g | Protein: 10g | Cholesterol: 7mg

## INGREDIENTS

- 2 cups uncooked orzo pasta
- 3/4 cup grated Parmesan cheese

- 1/2 cup chopped fresh basil leaves
- 1/3 cup chopped oil-packed sun-dried tomatoes
- 2 tablespoons olive oil
- 1/2 teaspoon salt
- 1/2 teaspoon ground black pepper

## DIRECTIONS

1. Bring a large pot of lightly salted water to a boil. Add orzo and cook for 8 to 10 minutes or until al dente. Drain and set aside.
2. Place basil leaves and sun-dried tomatoes in a food processor. Pulse 4 or 5 times until blended.
3. In a large bowl, toss together the orzo, basil-tomato mixture, olive oil, Parmesan cheese, salt and pepper. Serve warm or chilled.

# ALI'S GREEK TORTELLINI SALAD

**Servings: 8 | Prep: 15m | Cooks: 15m | Total: 2h30m | Additional: 2h**

## NUTRITION FACTS

Calories: 486 | Carbohydrates: 35.7g | Fat: 30.3g | Protein: 19.8g | Cholesterol: 196mg

## INGREDIENTS

- 2 (9 ounce) packages cheese tortellini
- 1/2 teaspoon salt
- ½ cup extra virgin olive oil
- 6 eggs
- 1/4 cup lemon juice
- 1 pound baby spinach leaves
- 1/4 cup red wine vinegar
- 1 cup crumbled feta cheese
- 2 tablespoons chopped fresh parsley
- 1/2 cup slivered red onion
- 1 teaspoon dried oregano

## DIRECTIONS

1. Bring a large pot of lightly salted water to a boil. Add tortellini, and cook for 7 minutes or until al dente; drain.
2. In a large bowl, mix the olive oil, lemon juice, red wine vinegar, parsley, oregano, and salt. Place the cooked tortellini in the bowl, and toss to coat. Cover, and chill at least 2 hours in the refrigerator.
3. Place eggs in a saucepan with enough water to cover, and bring to a boil. Remove from heat, and allow eggs to sit in the hot water for 10 to 12 minutes. Drain, cool, peel, and quarter.

4. Gently mix the spinach, feta cheese, and onion into the bowl with the pasta. Arrange the quartered eggs around the salad to serve.

# THAI-INSPIRED NOODLE SALAD
**Servings: 8 | Prep: 15m | Cooks: 10m | Total: 1h25**

## NUTRITION FACTS

Calories: 242 | Carbohydrates: 47.1g | Fat: 3.7g | Protein: 9.7g | Cholesterol: 0mg

## INGREDIENTS

- 15 ounces dried soba noodles
- 2 cloves garlic, minced
- 1 1/2 teaspoons dark sesame oil
- 2 teaspoons red pepper flakes, or to taste (optional)
- 1/3 cup rice vinegar
- 1 cup finely grated carrot
- 1/3 cup soy sauce
- 1/2 cup chopped fresh cilantro
- 1 lime, zested and juiced
- 1/4 cup coarsely chopped salted peanuts
- 2 tablespoons brown sugar

## DIRECTIONS

1. In a large pot, cook soba noodles according to package directions. Drain, rinse noodles with cold water, and set aside.
2. Pour sesame oil, rice vinegar, soy sauce, and lime juice into a large bowl. Mix in lime zest, brown sugar, garlic, and red pepper flakes; stir until sugar dissolves. Toss in carrots, cilantro, and peanuts.
3. Cut noodles into 3-inch lengths. Stir into dressing mixture. Cover, and refrigerate at least 1 hour.
4. Toss salad again before serving. If dry, splash with soy sauce and vinegar. Serve cold.

# ORZO AND TOMATO SALAD WITH FETA CHEESE
**Servings: 6 | Prep: 15m | Cooks: 10m | Total: 25m**

## NUTRITION FACTS

Calories: 329 | Carbohydrates: 28.1g | Fat: 19.6g | Protein: 10.9g | Cholesterol: 37mg

## INGREDIENTS

- 1 cup uncooked orzo pasta
- 1 ripe tomato, chopped

- 1/4 cup pitted green olives
- 1/4 cup virgin olive oil
- 1 cup diced feta cheese
- 1/8 cup lemon juice
- 3 tablespoons chopped fresh parsley
- salt and pepper to taste
- 3 tablespoons chopped fresh dill

## DIRECTIONS

1. Bring a large pot of lightly salted water to a boil. Cook orzo for 8 to 10 minutes, or until al dente; drain, and rinse with cold water.
2. When orzo is cool, transfer to a medium bowl and mix in olives, feta cheese, parsley, dill, and tomato. In a small bowl, whisk together oil and lemon juice. Pour over pasta, and mix well. Season with salt and pepper to taste. Chill before serving.

# PASTA SALAD

**Servings: 6 | Prep: 20m | Cooks: 15m | Total: 13h55m**

## NUTRITION FACTS

Calories: 400 | Carbohydrates: 39g | Fat: 24.8g | Protein: 7.9g | Cholesterol: 3mg

## INGREDIENTS

- 1 pound tri-colored spiral pasta
- 1 green bell pepper, chopped
- 6 tablespoons salad seasoning mix
- 1 red bell pepper, diced
- 1 (16 ounce) bottle Italian-style salad dressing
- 1/2 yellow bell pepper, chopped
- 2 cups cherry tomatoes, diced
- 1 (2.25 ounce) can black olives, chopped

## DIRECTIONS

1. In a large pot of salted boiling water, cook pasta until al dente, rinse under cold water and drain.
2. Whisk together the salad spice mix and Italian dressing.
3. In a salad bowl, combine the pasta, cherry tomatoes, bell peppers and olives. Pour dressing over salad; toss and refrigerate overnight.

# FROG EYE SALAD

**Servings: 10 | Prep: 15m | Cooks: 30m | Total: 14h5m**

## NUTRITION FACTS

Calories: 581 | Carbohydrates: 114.1g | Fat: 11g | Protein: 8.6g | Cholesterol: 37mg

## INGREDIENTS

- 1 cup white sugar
- 1 (16 ounce) package acini di pepe pasta
- 2 tablespoons all-purpose flour
- 3 (11 ounce) cans mandarin oranges, drained
- 2 1/2 teaspoons salt
- 2 (20 ounce) cans pineapple tidbits, drained
- 1 3/4 cups unsweetened pineapple juice
- 1 (20 ounce) can crushed pineapple, drained
- 2 eggs, beaten
- 1 (8 ounce) container frozen whipped topping, thawed
- 1 tablespoon lemon juice
- 1 cup miniature marshmallows
- 3 quarts water
- 1 cup shredded coconut
- 1 tablespoon vegetable oil

## DIRECTIONS

1. In a sauce pan, combine sugar, flour, 1/2 teaspoon salt, pineapple juice and eggs. Stir and cook over medium heat until thickened. Remove from heat; add lemon juice and cool to room temperature.
2. Bring water to a boil, add oil, remaining salt and cook pasta until al dente. Rinse under cold water and drain.
3. In a large bowl, combine the pasta, egg mixture, mandarin oranges, pineapple and whipped topping. Mix well and refrigerate overnight or until chilled. Before serving add marshmallows and coconut. Toss and serve.

# TORTELLINI BACON BROCCOLI SALAD

**Servings: 10 | Prep: 15m | Cooks: 15m | Total: 1h30m | Additional: 1h**

## NUTRITION FACTS

Calories: 348.8 | Carbohydrates: 33.6g | Fat: 0g | Protein: 13.9g | Cholesterol: 46.9mg

## INGREDIENTS

- 2 (9 ounce) packages refrigerated three-cheese tortellini
- 1 pint grape tomatoes, halved
- 1 pound bacon
- 2 eaches green onions, finely chopped

- 4 cups chopped broccoli
- 1 cup bottled coleslaw dressing

## DIRECTIONS

1. Cook the tortellini according to the package directions, drain, rinse with cold water, and refrigerate until cool, about 30 minutes.
2. Place the bacon in a large, deep skillet, and cook over medium-high heat, turning occasionally, until evenly browned, about 10 minutes. Drain the bacon slices on a paper towel-lined plate. Chop the bacon into 1/2-inch pieces while still a little warm.
3. Place the tortellini, bacon, broccoli, grape tomatoes, and green onions into a salad bowl. Pour the dressing over the ingredients, and toss lightly to coat. Chill in refrigerator before serving.

# SEAFOOD PASTA SALAD

**Servings: 8 | Prep: 25m | Cooks: 10m | Total: 5h35m**

## NUTRITION FACTS

Calories: 436 | Carbohydrates: 46.4g | Fat: 22.9g | Protein: 11.3g | Cholesterol: 22mg

## INGREDIENTS

- 1 1/2 (8 ounce) packages tri-color pasta
- 1 1/2 tablespoons white sugar
- 3 stalks celery
- 2 tablespoons white vinegar
- 1 pound imitation crabmeat
- 3 tablespoons milk
- 1 cup frozen green peas
- 1 teaspoon salt
- 1 cup mayonnaise
- 1/4 teaspoon ground black pepper

## DIRECTIONS

1. Bring a large pot of lightly salted water to a boil. Add pasta and cook for 8 to 10 minutes or until al dente; rinse under cold water until cool and drain.
2. While pasta is cooking, chop celery and crabmeat. Run hot water over peas to defrost.
3. In a large bowl, whisk together the mayonnaise, sugar, vinegar, milk, salt and pepper. Add the pasta, celery and crabmeat and stir until evenly coated. Adjust the salt, sugar or mayonnaise to suit your taste. Chill several hours before serving.

# PASTA SALAD WITH HOMEMADE DRESSING

**Servings: 8 | Prep: 35m | Cooks: 10m | Total: 8h45m | Additional: 8h**

## NUTRITION FACTS

Calories: 443 | Carbohydrates: 25.4g | Fat: 32g | Protein: 15.9g | Cholesterol: 39mg

## INGREDIENTS

- 1 (8 ounce) package uncooked tri-color rotini pasta
- 1/4 cup grated Parmesan cheese
- 6 ounces pepperoni sausage, diced
- 1/2 cup olive oil
- 6 ounces provolone cheese, cubed
- 1/4 cup red wine vinegar
- 1 red onion, thinly sliced
- 2 cloves garlic, minced
- 1 small cucumber, thinly sliced
- 1 teaspoon dried basil
- 3/4 cup chopped green bell pepper
- 1 teaspoon dried oregano
- 3/4 cup chopped red bell pepper
- 1/2 teaspoon ground mustard seed
- 1 (6 ounce) can pitted black olives
- 1/4 teaspoon salt
- 1/4 cup minced fresh parsley
- 1/8 teaspoon ground black pepper

## DIRECTIONS

1. Bring a large pot of lightly salted water to a boil. Add rotini pasta, and cook for 8 to 10 minutes, until al dente. Drain, and rinse with cold water.
2. In a large bowl, mix the cooled pasta, pepperoni, provolone cheese, red onion, cucumber, green bell pepper, red bell pepper, olives, parsley, and Parmesan cheese.
3. In a jar with a lid, mix the olive oil, vinegar, garlic, basil, oregano, ground mustard, salt, and pepper. Seal jar, and shake well.
4. Pour the dressing mixture over the pasta salad, and toss to coat. Cover, and chill 8 hours in the refrigerator.

# SESAME NOODLE SALAD

**Servings: 8 | Prep: 15m | Cooks: 5m | Total: 20m**

## NUTRITION FACTS

Calories: 338 | Carbohydrates: 40.8g | Fat: 16.8g | Protein: 7.3g | Cholesterol: 0mg

## INGREDIENTS

- 1 (16 ounce) package angel hair pasta
- 1/4 cup white sugar
- 1/2 cup sesame oil
- 1 teaspoon sesame seeds, or more if desired
- 1/2 cup soy sauce
- 1 green onion, chopped
- 1/4 cup balsamic vinegar
- 1 red bell pepper, diced
- 1 tablespoon hot chili oil

## DIRECTIONS

1. Fill a large pot with lightly salted water and bring to a rolling boil over high heat. Once the water is boiling, stir in the angel hair pasta, and return to a boil. Cook the pasta uncovered, stirring occasionally, until the pasta has cooked through, but is still firm to the bite, 4 to 5 minutes. Drain well in a colander set in the sink.
2. Whisk together the sesame oil, soy sauce, balsamic vinegar, chili oil, and sugar in a large bowl. Toss the pasta in the dressing, then sprinkle with sesame seeds, green onion, and bell pepper. Serve warm, or cover and refrigerate for a cold salad.

# AWESOME BOW TIE PASTA
### Servings: 8 | Prep: 7m | Cooks: 8m | Total: 15m

## NUTRITION FACTS

Calories: 338 | Carbohydrates: 46g | Fat: 12.9g | Protein: 11g | Cholesterol: 19mg

## INGREDIENTS

- 1 (16 ounce) package bow tie pasta
- 1/2 cup balsamic vinegar
- 2 green onions, chopped
- 1/4 cup extra virgin olive oil
- 1 (6 ounce) package feta cheese, crumbled
- 2 cups chopped fresh tomato

## DIRECTIONS

1. Bring a large pot of lightly salted water to a boil. Add pasta and cook for 8 to 10 minutes or until al dente; drain and place in ice water until cool.

2. Toss pasta with onion, feta, balsamic, olive oil and tomato. Serve immediately or chill 1 to 2 hours in refrigerator.

# CHICKEN CAESAR PASTA

**Servings: 8 | Prep: 30m | Cooks: 20m | Total: 50m**

## NUTRITION FACTS

Calories: 465 | Carbohydrates: 48.1g | Fat: 16.4g | Protein: 29g | Cholesterol: 63mg

## INGREDIENTS

- 1 pound dry penne pasta
- 1 (8 ounce) bottle Caesar salad dressing
- 1 tablespoon butter
- 1/4 cup red wine vinegar
- 6 skinless, boneless chicken breast halves - cut into 1 inch cubes
- 1/2 cup grated Parmesan cheese
- 1/2 teaspoon ground black pepper
- 1 head romaine lettuce - rinsed, dried and shredded
- 1/4 teaspoon salt
- 1 large tomato, chopped

## DIRECTIONS

1. Bring a large pot of lightly salted water to a boil. Add penne pasta and cook for 8 to 10 minutes or until al dente; drain.
2. Melt butter in a large skillet over medium heat. Add chicken, pepper and salt. Cook 10 minutes or until chicken is cooked through. Remove skillet from heat.
3. In a bowl, mix together salad dressing, vinegar and cheese. Toss together pasta, chicken, lettuce, and dressing mixture. Place in large serving bowl, and sprinkle with tomato. Garnish with croutons and Parmesan curls, if desired.

# KIM'S MACARONI SALAD

**Servings: 6 | Prep: 15m | Cooks: 15m | Total: 1h**

## NUTRITION FACTS

Calories: 352 | Carbohydrates: 31.1g | Fat: 22.7g | Protein: 5.8g | Cholesterol: 10mg

## INGREDIENTS

- 1 (8 ounce) package uncooked elbow macaroni
- 1 teaspoon kosher salt

- 3/4 cup mayonnaise
- 1/4 teaspoon white pepper
- 2 tablespoons cider vinegar
- 1/4 cup green onions, sliced
- 1 teaspoon sugar
- 2 jalapeno peppers, seeded and chopped

## DIRECTIONS

1. Bring a large pot of lightly salted water to a boil. Add macaroni, and cook until tender, about 8 minutes. Drain, and rinse under cold running water.
2. In a large bowl, mix together the mayonnaise, vinegar, sugar, salt, pepper, green onions and jalapeno peppers. Stir in the macaroni. Refrigerate until chilled before serving, at least 30 minutes.

# SPINACH BASIL PASTA SALAD
## Servings: 10 | Prep: 15m | Cooks: 15m | Total: 30m

## NUTRITION FACTS

Calories: 372 | Carbohydrates: 36.4g | Fat: 20.7g | Protein: 13.6g | Cholesterol: 15mg

## INGREDIENTS

- 1 (16 ounce) package bow tie pasta
- 4 ounces prosciutto, diced
- 1 (6 ounce) package spinach leaves
- salt and ground black pepper to taste
- 2 cups fresh basil leaves
- 3/4 cup freshly grated Parmesan cheese
- 1/2 cup extra virgin olive oil
- 1/2 cup toasted pine nuts
- 3 cloves garlic, minced

## DIRECTIONS

1. Fill a large pot with lightly salted water and bring to a rolling boil over high heat. Once the water is boiling, stir in the bow tie pasta and return to a boil. Cook the pasta uncovered, stirring occasionally, until the pasta has cooked through, but is still firm to the bite, about 12 minutes. Rinse with cold water to cool. Drain well in a colander set in the sink.
2. Toss the spinach and basil together in a large bowl.
3. Heat the olive oil in a skillet over medium heat; cook and stir the garlic in the hot oil for 1 minute; stir in the prosciutto and cook 2 to 3 minutes more. Remove from heat. Add to the bowl with the spinach and basil mixture; toss to combine. Pour in the drained pasta and retoss. Season with salt and pepper. Sprinkle with the Parmesan cheese and pine nuts to serve.

# AMERICAN-ITALIAN PASTA SALAD

**Servings: 20 | Prep: 30m | Cooks: 10m | Total: 8h40m**

## NUTRITION FACTS

Calories: 236 | Carbohydrates: 20.5g | Fat: 14.6g | Protein: 5.6g | Cholesterol: 17mg

## INGREDIENTS

- 1 (16 ounce) package fusilli pasta
- 2 (2 ounce) cans sliced black olives
- 1 cup mayonnaise
- 1 cup cubed Genoa salami
- 1 cup sour cream
- 3/4 cup chopped green onions
- 2 tablespoons milk
- 3/4 cup chopped celery
- 1 (.7 ounce) package dry Italian-style salad dressing mix
- 1/2 cup chopped fresh parsley
- 1 cup frozen petite peas, thawed

## DIRECTIONS

1. In a large pot of salted boiling water, cook pasta until al dente, rinse under cold water, and drain.
2. In a medium bowl, combine mayonnaise, sour cream, milk and Italian dressing mix. Whisk together until smooth, set aside.
3. In a large salad bowl combine cooked and cooled pasta, peas, olives, salami, green onions, celery and parsley. Mix in dressing last, reserving 1/2 cup. Let sit overnight in fridge. Stir before serving. Add extra dressing if pasta appears dry.

# ANTIPASTO SALAD

**Servings: 6 | Prep: 10m | Cooks: 15m | Total: 2h25m**

## NUTRITION FACTS

Calories: 415 | Carbohydrates: 25g | Fat: 29.6g | Protein: 12.6g | Cholesterol: 29mg

## INGREDIENTS

- 1/2 cup vegetable oil
- 6 ounces macaroni
- 3 tablespoons red wine vinegar
- 1/4 cup grated Parmesan cheese
- 1 clove garlic, minced

- 2 cups broccoli florets
- 1 teaspoon dried basil
- 4 ounces sliced pepperoni sausage
- 1/8 teaspoon crushed red pepper flakes
- 10 cherry tomatoes, halved
- 1 teaspoon salt
- 1/2 cup shredded mozzarella cheese

## DIRECTIONS

1. Cook pasta in a pot of boiling salted water until al dente. Drain.
2. In large bowl, stir together oil, vinegar, garlic, basil, and salt and pepper. Toss with warm macaroni to coat well. Toss with Parmesan. Cover, and refrigerate 2 to 3 hours.
3. Add broccoli, pepperoni, and tomatoes; toss well. Sprinkle with mozzarella cheese, and serve.

# MACARONI SALAD WITH PICKLES
### Servings: 6 | Prep: 15m | Cooks: 30m | Total: 45m

## NUTRITION FACTS

Calories: 689 | Carbohydrates: 66.7g | Fat: 40.3g | Protein: 16.2g | Cholesterol: 146mg

## INGREDIENTS

- 1 (16 ounce) package macaroni
- 2 tablespoons celery seed
- 4 eggs
- 1 cup chopped celery
- 1 cup mayonnaise
- 1/2 cup chopped red onion
- 1/2 cup sour cream
- 1/2 cup pimento-stuffed green olives
- 1 teaspoon salt, or to taste
- 1/4 cup chopped sweet pickle
- 1/4 teaspoon ground black pepper, or to taste
- 2 carrots, grated
- 1/4 teaspoon ground mustard
- 1 green bell pepper, chopped
- 2 tablespoons sweet pickle juice

## DIRECTIONS

1. Cook pasta in a large pot of boiling water until al dente. Drain; rinse with cold water. Set aside.

2. Meanwhile, place eggs in a saucepan, and fill with enough cold water to cover eggs completely by about 1 inch. Bring water to a boil. Cover, remove from heat, and let eggs stand in hot water for 20 minutes. Immediately remove from hot water and cool in an ice water bath. When cool enough to handle, peel and chop eggs.
3. In a medium bowl, mix together mayonnaise, sour cream, dry mustard, sweet pickle juice, and celery seed. Season with salt and black pepper.
4. In a large bowl, combine drained pasta, celery, onion, olives, sweet pickles, carrots, green pepper, and chopped eggs. Stir in dressing, and mix well. Refrigerate before serving.

# CRAB SALAD

**Servings: 8 | Prep: 25m | Cooks: 10m | Total: 35m**

## NUTRITION FACTS

Calories: 287 | Carbohydrates: 25.7g | Fat: 18.1g | Protein: 6.8g | Cholesterol: 16mg

## INGREDIENTS

- 1 1/2 cups seashell pasta
- 3/4 cup mayonnaise
- 1 (12 ounce) package imitation crabmeat
- 1 tablespoon white vinegar
- 1 small green bell pepper, diced
- 1 teaspoon lemon juice
- 1 sweet onion, diced
- 1/2 packet artificial sweetener
- 1/2 cup diced black olives
- 1/2 teaspoon garlic powder
- 5 radishes, diced
- 1/2 teaspoon dried dill weed
- 1 tomato, seeded and diced
- 1/2 teaspoon dried basil
- 1/2 cup diagonally sliced celery
- 1/2 teaspoon dried oregano

## DIRECTIONS

1. Bring a large pot of lightly salted water to a boil. Add pasta and cook for 8 to 10 minutes or until al dente; rinse with cold water and drain.
2. In a large bowl, whisk together the mayonnaise, vinegar, lemon juice, artificial sweetener, garlic powder, dill, basil and oregano, adjusting seasonings to suit your taste.
3. Add the pasta to the dressing and toss to coat. Add the crab, green pepper, onion, olives, radishes, tomato and celery and gently fold into the salad mixture. Cover and refrigerate until serving.

# ALLISON'S PASTA SALAD

**Servings: 8 | Prep: 15m | Cooks: 15m | Total: 30m**

## NUTRITION FACTS

Calories: 351 | Carbohydrates: 17.3g | Fat: 25.9g | Protein: 13.2g | Cholesterol: 55mg

## INGREDIENTS

- 1 3/4 cups farfalle pasta
- 1/4 teaspoon dried dill weed
- 1/2 cup mayonnaise
- 1/4 teaspoon salt
- 1/2 cup sour cream
- 2 cups seedless green grapes, halved
- 2 tablespoons cider vinegar
- 2 cups diced ham
- 1 1/2 tablespoons prepared Dijon-style mustard
- 1/2 cup chopped green onions
- 1 teaspoon white sugar
- 1 1/2 cups diced sharp Cheddar cheese
- 1/2 teaspoon ground black pepper

## DIRECTIONS

1. Cook pasta in a large pot of boiling water until al dente. Drain, and rinse in cold water.
2. In a small bowl, mix together mayonnaise, sour cream, cider vinegar, mustard, sugar, black pepper, dill weed, and salt.
3. In a large bowl, combine pasta, grapes, ham, green onions, and cheese. Toss with dressing. Cover, and chill overnight or for at least 6 hours.

# RAINBOW PASTA SALAD

**Servings: 8 | Prep: 15m | Cooks: 10m | Total: 1h25m | Additional: 1h**

## NUTRITION FACTS

Calories: 415 | Carbohydrates: 25.6g | Fat: 29.1g | Protein: 13.9g | Cholesterol: 33mg

## INGREDIENTS

- 1 (16 ounce) package tri-color rotini pasta
- 1 (6 ounce) can black olives, drained and sliced
- ¼ pound sliced pepperoni sausage
- 1 (8 ounce) package mozzarella cheese, shredded

- 1 cup fresh broccoli florets
- 1 (16 ounce) bottle Italian-style salad dressing

## DIRECTIONS

1. Bring a large pot of lightly salted water to a boil. Add pasta and cook for 8 to 10 minutes or until al dente; drain and rinse twice in cold water.
2. In a large bowl, combine cooked pasta, pepperoni, broccoli, olives, cheese and dressing.
3. Refrigerate for at least 1 hour before serving.

# COLD TUNA MACARONI SALAD
### Servings: 6 | Prep: 15m | Cooks: 15m | Total: 1h30m

## NUTRITION FACTS

Calories: 499 | Carbohydrates: 52.7g | Fat: 22g | Protein: 22.9g | Cholesterol: 38mg

## INGREDIENTS

- 1 (12 ounce) package macaroni
- 1 1/2 cups light mayonnaise
- 3 tomatoes - peeled, seeded and diced
- 1 tablespoon Italian-style salad dressing
- 3 stalks celery, chopped
- 1 tablespoon white sugar
- 1 (12 ounce) can tuna
- 1 pinch ground black pepper

## DIRECTIONS

1. In a large pot of salted boiling water, cook pasta until al dente, rinse under cold water and drain.
2. In a large bowl, combine the pasta, tomatoes, celery and tuna.
3. Prepare the dressing by whisking together the mayonnaise, salad dressing, sugar and pepper. Add to pasta salad, mix together, and refrigerate for 1 hour.

# THE PASTA SALAD
### Servings: 7 | Prep: 15m | Cooks: 25m | Total: 8h55m

## NUTRITION FACTS

Calories: 450 | Carbohydrates: 31.9g | Fat: 27.7g | Protein: 19.5g | Cholesterol: 99mg

## INGREDIENTS

- 1 (8 ounce) package small seashell pasta
- 1/4 cup sour cream
- 2 eggs
- green onions, chopped
- 2 ounces cooked ham, cut into thin strips
- 1 teaspoon prepared mustard
- 1 (10 ounce) package frozen English peas, thawed
- 1 teaspoon hot pepper sauce
- 1 cup shredded Swiss cheese
- 1 teaspoon paprika
- 1/2 cup mayonnaise

## DIRECTIONS

1. Bring a large pot of lightly salted water to a boil. Add pasta and cook for 8 to 10 minutes, or until al dente. Rinse under cold water, drain, and set aside.
2. Meanwhile, place eggs in a saucepan and cover with cold water. Over medium heat, bring water to a full boil. Lower heat and simmer for 10 to 15 minutes. Immediately plunge eggs into cold water. Let cool completely, then peel and slice.
3. In a large serving bowl, toss together the pasta, egg, ham, peas, and Swiss cheese. In a separate bowl, mix together the mayonnaise, sour cream, green onion, mustard, mustard, and hot pepper sauce. Stir until well blended.
4. Pour 3/4 of the dressing over the pasta, and toss to coat thoroughly. Spread the remaining dressing evenly over the top of the pasta salad, all the way to the edge of the bowl. Sprinkle with paprika, cover tightly, and chill 4 hours, or overnight for best flavor.

# TORTELLINI SALAD
### Servings: 8 | Prep: 20m | Cooks: 5m | Total: 1h25m

## NUTRITION FACTS

Calories: 415 | Carbohydrates: 30.3g | Fat: 25.9g | Protein: 17g | Cholesterol: 53mg

## INGREDIENTS

- 1 (16 ounce) package refrigerated cheese tortellini
- 1/3 cup extra-virgin olive oil
- 4 ounces sliced pepperoni, quartered
- 1 1/2 tablespoons balsamic vinegar
- 2 green onions, sliced
- 1 1/2 tablespoons distilled white vinegar
- 1 (2.25 ounce) can sliced black olives
- 1 teaspoon dried Italian herb seasoning
- 1 (6.5 ounce) jar marinated artichoke hearts, drained and chopped

- salt and black pepper to taste
- 6 ounces mozzarella cheese, diced

## DIRECTIONS

1. Cook the tortellini according to package instructions, drain in a colander set in the sink, and rinse with cold water.
2. Place the tortellini, pepperoni, green onions, olives, artichoke hearts, and mozzarella cheese in a large salad bowl.
3. Whisk together the olive oil, balsamic vinegar, white vinegar, Italian seasonings, and salt and pepper in a bowl, and pour over the salad ingredients. Gently stir to combine, and refrigerate to chill before serving. For even better flavor, let chill in refrigerator for at least 2 hours before serving.

# SHRIMP AND PASTA SHELL SALAD
### Servings: 8 | Prep: 25m | Cooks: 10m | Total: 2h35m

## NUTRITION FACTS

Calories: 451 | Carbohydrates: 33.8g | Fat: 28.8g | Protein: 15.4g | Cholesterol: 99mg

## INGREDIENTS

- 1 1/4 cups mayonnaise, or more if needed
- 1 (12 ounce) package small pasta shells
- 2 teaspoons Dijon mustard
- 1 pound cooked, peeled, and deveined small shrimp - cut in half
- 2 teaspoons ketchup
- 1/2 cup finely diced red bell pepper
- 1/4 teaspoon Worcestershire sauce
- 3/4 cup diced celery
- 1 teaspoon salt, or to taste
- salt and ground black pepper to taste
- 1 pinch cayenne pepper, or to taste
- 1 pinch paprika, for garnish
- 1 lemon, juiced
- 3 sprigs fresh dill, or as desired
- 1/3 cup chopped fresh dill

## DIRECTIONS

1. Whisk 1 1/4 cup mayonnaise, Dijon mustard, ketchup, Worcestershire sauce, salt, and cayenne pepper together in a bowl; add lemon juice and 1/3 cup chopped dill. Whisk until thoroughly combined. Refrigerate.
2. Bring a pot of well-salted water to a boil and stir in pasta shells; cook until tender, 8 to 10 minutes. Drain and rinse with cold water to cool pasta slightly; drain again. Transfer to a large bowl.

3. Toss shrimp with pasta; add red bell pepper, celery, and dressing to pasta and shrimp. Mix thoroughly to coat and fill shells with dressing. Cover bowl with plastic wrap and refrigerate until chilled, 2 to 3 hours.
4. Stir salad again before serving and season to taste with more salt, black pepper, lemon juice, and cayenne pepper if desired. If salad seems a little dry, mix in a little more mayonnaise. Garnish with paprika and sprigs of dill.

# PESTO PASTA CAPRESE SALAD
**Servings: 6 | Prep: 10m | Cooks: 10m | Total: 20m**

## NUTRITION FACTS

Calories: 169 | Carbohydrates: 17.1g | Fat: 8.3g | Protein: 6.1g | Cholesterol: 10mg

## INGREDIENTS

- 1 1/2 cups rotini pasta
- 1/8 teaspoon ground black pepper
- 3 tablespoons pesto, or to taste
- 1/2 cup halved grape tomatoes
- 1 tablespoon extra-virgin olive oil
- 1/2 cup small (pearlini) fresh mozzarella balls
- 1/4 teaspoon salt, or to taste
- 2 leaves fresh basil leaves, finely shredded
- 1/4 teaspoon granulated garlic

## DIRECTIONS

1. Bring a large pot of lightly salted water to a boil; cook the rotini at a boil until tender yet firm to the bite, about 8 minutes; drain.
2. Mix pesto, olive oil, salt, granulated garlic, and black pepper in a bowl; add rotini. Toss to coat. Fold in tomatoes, mozzarella, and fresh basil.

# ASPARAGUS, FETA AND COUSCOUS SALAD
**Servings: 4 | Prep: 10m | Cooks: 20m | Total: 30m**

## NUTRITION FACTS

Calories: 541 | Carbohydrates: 77.7g | Fat: 16.7g | Protein: 20.1g | Cholesterol: 38mg

## INGREDIENTS

- 2 cups couscous
- 3 tablespoons balsamic vinegar

- 1 bunch fresh asparagus, trimmed and cut into 2-inch pieces
- 2 tablespoons extra-virgin olive oil
- 8 ounces grape tomatoes, halved
- Black pepper, to taste
- 6 ounces feta cheese, crumbled

## DIRECTIONS

1. Cook couscous according to package instructions. Put aside and allow to cool slightly.
2. Meanwhile, place asparagus in a steamer over 1 inch of boiling water, and cover. Cook until tender but still firm, about 2 to 6 minutes. Drain and cool.
3. Toss the asparagus, tomatoes, and feta with couscous. Add the olive oil, balsamic vinegar, and black pepper and toss to incorporate.

# BUFFALO CHICKEN PASTA SALAD

**Servings: 12 | Prep: 20m | Cooks: 10m | Total: 1h30m | Additional: 1h**

## NUTRITION FACTS

Calories: 379 | Carbohydrates: 34.6g | Fat: 21.1g | Protein: 13.6g | Cholesterol: 40mg

## INGREDIENTS

- 1 (16 ounce) package uncooked rotini pasta
- 1/2 teaspoon black pepper
- 1/2 cup mayonnaise
- 1 pound frozen cooked chicken strips, defrosted and diced
- 1 cup chunky blue cheese dressing
- 1/2 cup red bell pepper, diced
- 1/2 cup buffalo wing sauce
- 1/2 cup green bell pepper, diced
- 1 teaspoon salt
- 1 cup red onion, diced

## DIRECTIONS

1. Fill a large pot with lightly salted water and bring to a rolling boil over high heat. Once the water is boiling, stir in the rotini, and return to a boil. Cook uncovered, stirring occasionally, until the pasta has cooked through, but is still firm to the bite, about 8 minutes. Drain well in a colander set in the sink.
2. Stir together the mayonnaise, blue cheese dressing, buffalo wing sauce, salt and pepper in a large bowl. Add the chicken, bell peppers, red onion, and cooked pasta and toss to coat with the dressing. Cover and chill at least 1 hour in the refrigerator before serving.

# COLD MACARONI AND TUNA SALAD

**Servings: 6 | Prep: 25m | Cooks: 18m | Total: 1h58m**

## NUTRITION FACTS

Calories: 342 | Carbohydrates: 40.8g | Fat: 9.5g | Protein: 22.1g | Cholesterol: 108mg

## INGREDIENTS

- 3 eggs
- 3 tablespoons mayonnaise
- 2 3/4 cups macaroni
- 1/4 teaspoon salt
- 1/2 (10 ounce) package frozen English peas
- 1/8 teaspoon ground black pepper
- 2 (5 ounce) cans tuna, drained

## DIRECTIONS

1. Place eggs in a saucepan and cover with water. Bring to a boil, remove from heat, and let eggs stand in hot water for 15 minutes. Remove eggs from hot water, cool under cold running water, and peel.
2. Bring a large pot of lightly salted water to a boil. Add macaroni pasta and cook for 8 to 10 minutes or until al dente; drain and rinse under cold water.
3. Put frozen peas into a colander and rinse with hot water; drain well.
4. Place the macaroni and peas in a large bowl. Dice eggs and add to the bowl. Put the tuna in the bowl, flaking it apart.
5. Stir mayonnaise into the mixture a little at a time, so the mixture is moist but not soggy. Sprinkle the salt and pepper and mix one last time. Cover and refrigerate for a least 1 hour or overnight.

# BEST CHICKEN PASTA SALAD

**Servings: 8 | Prep: 15m | Cooks: 35m | Total: 3h | Additional: 2h10m**

## NUTRITION FACTS

Calories: 476 | Carbohydrates: 43.6g | Fat: 25.5g | Protein: 20.3g | Cholesterol: 42mg

## INGREDIENTS

- 2 boneless, skinless chicken breast halves
- 1 Vidalia onion, diced
- 3/4 cup steak sauce
- 2 avocados - peeled, pitted and diced
- 1 (12 ounce) package fusilli pasta
- 1 cup halved cherry tomatoes
- 2 cubes chicken bouillon

- 1 cup Ranch-style salad dressing

## DIRECTIONS

1. Preheat an outdoor grill for high heat. Place breasts into a glass baking dish and marinate in steak sauce for 15 to 60 minutes.
2. Grill chicken until no longer pink and the juices run clear. Remove from grill, and chop into bite-size pieces.
3. To a large pot of boiling water, add bouillon cubes and pasta. Cook pasta until al dente. Drain, and rinse under cold water.
4. In a large bowl, combine chicken, pasta, onion, avocados and tomatoes. Mix in salad dressing, cover, and refrigerate until chilled.

# CHICKEN CASHEW SALAD
### Servings: 6 | Prep: 15m | Cooks: 10m | Total: 25m

## NUTRITION FACTS

Calories: 499 | Carbohydrates: 53g | Fat: 23.6g | Protein: 20.6g | Cholesterol: 45mg

## INGREDIENTS

- 2 cups seashell pasta
- 2 cups chopped celery
- 1/4 cup brown sugar
- 1/2 cup chopped green bell pepper
- 1 cup creamy salad dressing (e.g. Miracle Whip)
- 1 onion, chopped
- 2 teaspoons lemon juice
- 3 boneless chicken breast halves, cooked and cut into bite-sized pieces
- 1 tablespoon distilled white vinegar
- 1 cup cashew halves
- 1 pinch salt

## DIRECTIONS

1. Bring a large pot of lightly salted water to a boil. Add pasta and cook for 8 to 10 minutes or until al dente; drain and rinse with cold water.
2. In large bowl, combine brown sugar, salad dressing, lemon juice, vinegar and salt. Toss dressing mixture with cooked pasta, celery, green pepper, onion and chicken. Chill until ready to serve. Mix in cashews just before serving.

# GREEK PASTA SALAD WITH SHRIMP, TOMATOES, ZUCCHINI, PEPPERS, AND FETA

**Servings: 6 | Prep: 35m | Cooks: 17m | Total: 1h22m | Additional: 30m**

## NUTRITION FACTS

Calories: 802 | Carbohydrates: 65.8g | Fat: 45.7g | Protein: 33.6g | Cholesterol: 185mg

## INGREDIENTS

- 1/4 cup rice wine vinegar
- Big pinch of salt
- 2 tablespoons Dijon mustard
- Black pepper, to taste
- 1 large clove garlic, minced
- 2/3 cup extra-virgin olive oil
- 2 medium zucchini, thinly sliced lengthwise
- 1 pound cooked shrimp, halved lengthwise
- 1 medium yellow pepper, halved lengthwise, seeded
- 8 ounces cherry tomatoes, halved
- 2 tablespoons olive oil
- 3/4 cup coarsely chopped, pitted Kalamata olives
- Ground black pepper and salt, to taste
- 1 cup crumbled feta cheese
- 1 gallon water
- 1/2 small red onion, cut into small dice
- 2 tablespoons salt
- 2 teaspoons dried oregano
- 1 pound medium pasta shells

## DIRECTIONS

1. To make the vinaigrette, whisk together the rice wine vinegar, mustard, garlic, pinch of salt, and pepper; slowly pour in 2/3 cup olive oil, whisking constantly. Pour into a jar with a tight-fitting lid to transport it to the picnic.
2. Adjust oven rack to highest position and turn broiler on high. Toss zucchini and bell pepper with 2 tablespoons olive oil and salt and pepper to taste, and arrange on a large baking sheet with sides. Broil until spotty brown, 8 to 10 minutes, turning zucchini slices and pepper halves once. Set aside in a large bowl to cool, then cut into bite-sized pieces.
3. Bring 1 gallon of water and 2 tablespoons of salt to boil. Add pasta; boil using package times, until just tender. Drain thoroughly (do not rinse) and dump onto the baking sheet. Set aside to cool.
4. Put vegetables, pasta and remaining ingredients (except dressing) in the bowl or a gallon-sized zipper bag (can be refrigerated for several hours). When ready to serve, add dressing; toss to coat.

# TORTELLINI, STEAK, AND CAESAR
**Servings: 4 | Prep: 15m | Cooks: 15m | Total: 30m**

## NUTRITION FACTS

Calories: 671 | Carbohydrates: 46.6g | Fat: 42.1g | Protein: 27.8g | Cholesterol: 83mg

## INGREDIENTS

- 1 (9 ounce) package cheese tortellini
- 2 heads romaine lettuce, torn into bite-size pieces
- 1 pound flank steak
- 2 (2.25 ounce) cans small pitted black olives, drained
- garlic powder to taste
- 1 cup Caesar-style croutons
- salt and pepper to taste
- 2 small fresh tomatoes, chopped
- 1 tablespoon olive oil
- 1 (8 ounce) bottle Caesar salad dressing

## DIRECTIONS

1. Bring a large pot of lightly salted water to a boil. Place pasta in the pot, cook for 7 to 9 minutes, until al dente, and drain.
2. Preheat the oven broiler. Season steak with garlic powder, salt, and pepper; rub with olive oil. Place steak in a baking dish, and broil 5 minutes on each side, or to desired doneness. Slice diagonally into thin strips.
3. In a bowl, toss the cooked tortellini, lettuce, olives, croutons, tomatoes, and dressing. Top with steak strips to serve.

# RAINBOW PASTA SALAD
**Servings: 8 | Prep: 15m | Cooks: 10m | Total: 1h25m**

## NUTRITION FACTS

Calories: 387 | Carbohydrates: 51.7g | Fat: 16.7g | Protein: 8.3g | Cholesterol: 0mg

## INGREDIENTS

- 1 (16 ounce) package tri-colored pasta assortment
- 1 red onion, finely chopped
- 2 large tomatoes, diced
- 1 (16 ounce) bottle Italian-style salad dressing
- 1 large cucumber, peeled and diced

## DIRECTIONS

1. Bring a large pot of lightly salted water to a boil. Add pasta and cook for 8 to 10 minutes or until al dente; drain and rinse in cold water.
2. In a large bowl combine tomatoes, cucumbers, onion, cooled pasta and Italian dressing. Refrigerate overnight, or for at least 1 hour.

# AMELIA'S TUNA MACARONI SALAD
### Servings: 6 | Prep: 20m | Cooks: 0m | Total: 20m

## NUTRITION FACTS

Calories: 582 | Carbohydrates: 51.6g | Fat: 33.4g | Protein: 18.7g | Cholesterol: 126mg

## INGREDIENTS

- 1 (12 ounce) package elbow macaroni
- 1 cup mayonnaise
- 1 (5 ounce) can tuna, drained
- 2 tablespoons sweet pickle relish
- 2 stalks celery, chopped
- salt and pepper to taste
- 2 tablespoons chopped sweet onion
- 3 hard-cooked eggs, quartered
- 1 (10 ounce) can baby peas, drained
- 1 pinch paprika, for garnish

## DIRECTIONS

1. Bring a large pot of lightly salted water to a boil. Add the macaroni, and cook until tender, about 8 minutes. Drain and rinse under cold running water.
2. In a large bowl, stir together the macaroni, tuna, celery, onion and peas. Mix in the mayonnaise, relish, salt and pepper. Garnish with egg wedges and a sprinkle of paprika. Cover and chill for at least 1 hour before serving.

# SIMPLE PASTA SALAD
### Servings: 12 | Prep: 15m | Cooks: 12m | Total: 30m

## NUTRITION FACTS

Calories: 289 | Carbohydrates: 34.6g | Fat: 13.9g | Protein: 10g | Cholesterol: 8mg

## INGREDIENTS

- 1 (16 ounce) package uncooked rotini pasta
- 1 bunch green onions, chopped
- 1 (16 ounce) bottle Italian salad dressing
- 4 ounces grated Parmesan cheese
- 2 cucumbers, chopped
- 1 tablespoon Italian seasoning
- 6 tomatoes, chopped

## DIRECTIONS

1. Bring a large pot of lightly salted water to a boil. Place pasta in the pot, cook for 8 to 12 minutes, until al dente, and drain.
2. In a large bowl, toss the cooked pasta with the Italian dressing, cucumbers, tomatoes, and green onions. In a small bowl, mix the Parmesan cheese and Italian seasoning, and gently mix into the salad. Cover, and refrigerate until serving.

# BEST EVER PASTA SALAD
### Servings: 10 | Prep: 20m | Cooks: 10m | Total: 35m

## NUTRITION FACTS

Calories: 538 | Carbohydrates: 37.6g | Fat: 40.9g | Protein: 7.7g | Cholesterol: 27mg

## INGREDIENTS

- 1 (16 ounce) package dry penne pasta
- 1 (8 ounce) container sour cream
- 2 large cucumbers, peeled and cubed
- 3 tablespoons dried dill weed
- 2 roma (plum) tomatoes, chopped
- 2 tablespoons lemon pepper
- 2 cups mayonnaise

## DIRECTIONS

1. Bring a large pot of lightly salted water to a boil. Add penne pasta and cook for 8 to 10 minutes or until al dente; drain.
2. Combine pasta, cucumbers, tomatoes, mayonnaise, sour cream, dill weed and lemon pepper. Serve as is or chill for 45 minutes.

# REFRESHING SUMMER ORZO SALAD
### Servings: 8 | Prep: 20m | Cooks: 15m | Total: 35m

## NUTRITION FACTS

Calories: 553 | Carbohydrates: 49.6g | Fat: 32.3g | Protein: 19.3g | Cholesterol: 44mg

## INGREDIENTS

- 4 cups chicken broth
- 1/4 teaspoon crushed red pepper flakes
- 1 (16 ounce) package orzo pasta
- 1 cup pine nuts
- 1 1/2 tablespoons butter
- 1 cup pitted kalamata olives
- 1/4 cup extra-virgin olive oil
- 1 (2 ounce) jar capers, with liquid
- 1 1/2 teaspoons minced garlic
- 12 ounces basil-flavored feta cheese
- 1/2 teaspoon dried basil
- 1 (10 ounce) bag fresh spinach leaves, chopped
- 1/2 teaspoon dried thyme
- 1 tablespoon lemon juice

## DIRECTIONS

1. Bring the chicken broth to a boil over high heat. Add the orzo pasta, and cook until al dente, 8 to 10 minutes. Drain well, then pour the orzo into a bowl, and toss with the butter to keep it from sticking; set aside.
2. While the pasta is cooking, heat the olive oil in a skillet over medium heat. Stir in the garlic, and cook until the garlic softens and the aroma mellows, about 2 minutes. Stir in the basil, thyme, red pepper flakes, and pine nuts. Cook and stir until the pine nuts have toasted to a light golden brown.
3. Stir the pine nut mixture into the orzo along with the olives, capers, feta cheese, spinach, and lemon juice. Serve either warm or cold, but it's better the next day.

# SIMPLE MACARONI SALAD

### Servings: 8 | Prep: 20m | Cooks: 10m | Total: 2h30m

## NUTRITION FACTS

Calories: 436 | Carbohydrates: 45.8g | Fat: 24.5g | Protein: 8.1g | Cholesterol: 10mg

## INGREDIENTS

- 1 (16 ounce) package macaroni
- 1 stalk celery, chopped (optional)
- 2 red bell peppers, chopped
- 1 tablespoon olive oil
- 1 green bell pepper, chopped

- 1 cup mayonnaise
- 1/2 cup chopped green onions
- 1 packet dry vegetable soup mix

## DIRECTIONS

1. Bring a large pot of lightly salted water to a boil. Add pasta and cook for 8 to 10 minutes, or until al dente. Drain, and rinse with cold water until no longer hot. Transfer noodles to a large bowl.
2. Stir in red bell peppers, green bell peppers, green onions, celery and olive oil. Mix in mayonnaise and soup mix. Refrigerate for a few hours before serving.

# JIM'S MACARONI SALAD
### Servings: 9 | Prep: 30m | Cooks: 10m | Total: 40m

## NUTRITION FACTS

Calories: 488 | Carbohydrates: 43.3g | Fat: 29.1g | Protein: 13.6g | Cholesterol: 117mg

## INGREDIENTS

- 1 (16 ounce) package macaroni
- 1/2 cup chopped green bell pepper
- 1 tablespoon cider vinegar
- 6 slices American processed cheese, cut into 1/2-inch piece
- 1 cup mayonnaise
- 1 (6 ounce) can pitted ripe olives, drained
- 1/2 cup chopped white onion
- 4 hard-cooked eggs, chopped
- 1 (4 ounce) jar sliced pimento peppers, drained
- salt and ground black pepper to taste
- 1/2 cup chopped dill pickles

## DIRECTIONS

1. Cook the macaroni in a large pot of lightly salted boiling water until tender, 6-8 minutes depending on size. Drain, and set aside.
2. Stir the vinegar and mayonnaise together in a bowl until thoroughly blended.
3. Combine the cooked noodles, onions, pimentos, pickles, bell peppers, cheese, olives, and eggs in a large bowl. Add the mayonnaise mixture, and toss gently to coat ingredients. Season with salt and pepper to taste. Refrigerate until ready to serve.

# PENNE, TOMATO, AND MOZZARELLA SALAD
### Servings: 6 | Prep: 20m | Cooks: 20m | Total: 40m

Calories: 405 | Carbohydrates: 47.5g | Fat: 17.2g | Protein: 17.5g | Cholesterol: 21mg

## INGREDIENTS

- 1 (12 ounce) package penne pasta
- salt and pepper to taste
- 1/4 cup olive oil
- 5 ounces mozzarella cheese, diced
- 1 bunch green onions, chopped
- 1/2 cup grated Parmesan cheese
- 1 clove garlic, minced
- 4 ounces fresh basil
- 1 cup quartered cherry tomatoes
- 12 large black olives, halved

## DIRECTIONS

1. Cook pasta in a large pot of boiling salted water as directed on package, until just tender. Drain, and set aside.
2. Heat olive oil in a small saucepan. Add green onions and cook, stirring occasionally, 2 or 3 minutes. Stir in garlic, and cook for 2 minutes. Add pasta, tomatoes, salt, and pepper. Cook over low heat to warm through. Stir in mozzarella and Parmesan cheese. Coarsely tear basil leaves in halves or thirds; add to pasta with olives, and serve immediately.

# COUSCOUS AND CUCUMBER SALAD
### Servings: 8 | Prep: 10m | Cooks: 10m | Total: 1h20m

## NUTRITION FACTS

Calories: 142 | Carbohydrates: 24.6g | Fat: 3.6g | Protein: 4g | Cholesterol: 0mg

## INGREDIENTS

- 10 ounces uncooked couscous
- 1/2 cup finely chopped green onions
- 2 tablespoons olive oil
- 1/2 cup fresh parsley, chopped
- 1/2 cup lemon juice
- 1/4 cup fresh basil, chopped
- 3/4 teaspoon salt
- 6 leaves lettuce
- 1/4 teaspoon ground black pepper

- 6 slices lemon
- 1 cucumber, seeded and chopped

## DIRECTIONS

1. In a medium saucepan, bring 1 3/4 cup water to a boil. Stir in couscous; cover. Remove from heat; let stand, covered, 5 minutes. Cool to room temperature.
2. Meanwhile, in a medium bowl combine oil, lemon juice, salt and pepper. Stir in cucumber, green onion, parsley, basil and couscous. Mix well and chill for at least 1 hour.
3. Line a plate with lettuce leaves. Spoon couscous mixture over leaves and garnish with lemon wedges.

# TUNA PASTA SALAD WITH DILL
### Servings: 12 | Prep: 15m | Cooks: 10m | Total: 1h25m

## NUTRITION FACTS

Calories: 378 | Carbohydrates: 30.9g | Fat: 23.1g | Protein: 11.5g | Cholesterol: 18mg

## INGREDIENTS

- 1 (16 ounce) package small uncooked seashell pasta
- 1 teaspoon salt
- 1 1/2 cups mayonnaise
- 1/8 teaspoon ground black pepper
- 1/2 cup milk
- 2 (5 ounce) cans tuna packed in water, drained
- 2 tablespoons pickle juice
- 1/2 cup chopped onion (optional)
- 2 teaspoons dried dill weed

## DIRECTIONS

1. Bring a large pot of lightly salted water to a boil. Place pasta in the pot, cook for 8 to 10 minutes, until al dente, and drain.
2. In a large bowl, whisk together the mayonnaise, milk, pickle juice, dill, salt, and pepper. Mix in tuna and onion. Toss with cooked pasta. Cover and refrigerate 1 to 2 hours before serving.

# QUICK GREEK PASTA SALAD WITH STEAK
### Servings: 4 | Prep: 15m | Cooks: 20m | Total: 35m

## NUTRITION FACTS

Calories: 579 | Carbohydrates: 44.7g | Fat: 35g | Protein: 24.5g | Cholesterol: 73mg

## INGREDIENTS

- 8 ounces whole wheat penne pasta
- 1 tablespoon soy sauce
- 2 tablespoons extra virgin olive oil
- 1/2 cup sun-dried tomato pesto
- 1 tablespoon butter
- 1/2 cup sliced black olives
- 1 (1 pound) beef rib eye steak
- 1 cup chopped fresh spinach
- 1 tablespoon butter
- 1 teaspoon basil
- 1 teaspoon minced garlic
- 1 tablespoon chopped parsley
- 1/4 cup chopped shallots
- 1/2 cup crumbled feta cheese
- 3 tablespoons sunflower kernels

## DIRECTIONS

1. Bring a large pot of lightly salted water to a boil. Add pasta and cook for 8 to 10 minutes or until al dente. When cooked, drain, then toss with olive oil, and keep warm.
2. Meanwhile, melt 1 tablespoon butter in a skillet over medium-high heat. Sear the rib-eye on both sides until rosy-pink in the center, 7 to 10 minutes depending on thickness. Remove steak from skillet and cut into bite-size pieces. Melt the remaining 1 tablespoon of butter in the skillet, and stir in the garlic and shallots. Cook 5 to 10 seconds until fragrant, then return the steak to the pan and cook for another 5 minutes or to desired doneness. Stir in the soy sauce, and cook a few seconds longer, allowing it to evaporate.
3. Remove the skillet from the heat and stir in the sun-dried tomato pesto, olives, spinach, basil, parsley, feta cheese and sunflower kernels. Toss with the pasta in a large bowl and serve.

# SPAGHETTI SALAD
### Servings: 12 | Prep: 20m | Cooks: 10m | Total: 2h30m

## NUTRITION FACTS

Calories: 269 | Carbohydrates: 35.2g | Fat: 12g | Protein: 6g | Cholesterol: <1mg

## INGREDIENTS

- 1 pound spaghetti, broken into pieces
- 1/2 teaspoon garlic powder
- 1 (16 ounce) bottle Italian-style salad dressing

- 1/2 teaspoon ground black pepper
- 1 tablespoon grated Parmesan cheese
- 1/2 teaspoon cayenne pepper
- 1 tablespoon sesame seeds
- 1 cucumber, chopped
- 1 tablespoon poppy seeds
- 1 red onion, diced
- 2 teaspoons seasoning salt
- 2 tomatoes, chopped
- 1 teaspoon paprika

## DIRECTIONS

1. Cook spaghetti according to package directions. Drain, rinse with cold water and drain well. Transfer to large bowl.
2. In medium bowl, whisk together salad dressing, cheese, seeds, salt, paprika, garlic powder and peppers until well blended. Stir in cucumber and onion. Pour mixture over spaghetti and toss lightly to coat evenly. Cover and refrigerate for at least 2 hours or up to 24 hours. Top with tomatoes to serve.

# TORTELLINI SALAD

### Servings: 8 | Prep: 15m | Cooks: 15m | Total: 4h30m | Additional: 4h

## NUTRITION FACTS

Calories: 286 | Carbohydrates: 21.5g | Fat: 19.2g | Protein: 8.2g | Cholesterol: 19mg

## INGREDIENTS

- 16 ounces cheese-filled tortellini
- 1 tablespoon chopped fresh basil
- 1 red bell pepper, thinly sliced
- 1 tablespoon chopped fresh parsley
- 1/2 cup chopped green bell pepper
- 3 tablespoons lemon juice
- 1 onion, thinly sliced
- salt and pepper to taste
- 1/4 cup black olives, pitted and sliced
- 1/2 teaspoon garlic powder
- 1/2 cup vinegar
- 1 dash hot pepper sauce
- 1/2 cup olive oil
- 1/2 cup crumbled feta cheese

- 1 tablespoon chopped fresh mint
- 3 tablespoons grated Parmesan cheese

## DIRECTIONS

1. Cook pasta in a large pot of boiling water until al dente.
2. In a jar, combine vinegar, olive oil, fresh herbs, lemon juice, garlic powder, and hot sauce. Seal, and shake until well mixed. Season to taste with salt and black pepper.
3. In a large bowl combine, tortellini, peppers, onion, and olives. Pour lemon dressing over salad, and toss to coat pasta. Cover, and chill for at least four hours. Before serving, toss in feta and Parmesan.

# QUICK ITALIAN PASTA SALAD
### Servings: 12 | Prep: 15m | Cooks: 10m | Total: 25m

## NUTRITION FACTS

Calories: 371 | Carbohydrates: 29.2g | Fat: 21g | Protein: 15.2g | Cholesterol: 46mg

## INGREDIENTS

- 1 (12 ounce) package tri-color rotini pasta
- 1 cup Italian-style salad dressing
- 3/4 pound Italian salami, finely diced
- 1 (6 ounce) can sliced black olives
- 1/2 green bell pepper, sliced
- 8 ounces small fresh mozzarella balls (ciliegine)
- 1/2 red bell pepper, sliced
- 3 (.7 ounce) packages dry Italian-style salad dressing mix, or to taste
- 1/2 red onion, chopped
- 1/2 cup shredded Parmesan cheese

## DIRECTIONS

1. Bring a large pot of lightly salted water to a boil; cook rotini at a boil until tender yet firm to the bite, about 8 minutes; drain and rinse with cold water until cool.
2. Combine pasta, salami, green bell pepper, red bell pepper, onion, salad dressing, olives, and mozzarella cheese in a large bowl. Mix dry salad dressing into pasta; sprinkle with Parmesan cheese.

# SWEET PASTA SALAD
### Servings: 10 | Prep: 4h | Cooks: 10m | Total: 4h10m

## NUTRITION FACTS

Calories: 605 | Carbohydrates: 60.4g | Fat: 38.8g | Protein: 6.6g | Cholesterol: 30mg

## INGREDIENTS

- 1 pound rotini pasta
- 1 cup white sugar
- 4 carrots, shredded
- 1 (14 ounce) can sweetened condensed milk
- 1 green bell pepper, chopped
- 2 cups mayonnaise
- 1 onion, diced
- 1 teaspoon salt
- 1 cup distilled white vinegar
- 1/2 teaspoon ground black pepper

## DIRECTIONS

1. Bring a large pot of lightly salted water to a boil. Add pasta and cook for 8 to 10 minutes or until al dente; drain.
2. In large bowl, combine pasta, carrot, green pepper and onion. In medium bowl, combine vinegar, sugar, condensed milk, mayonnaise, salt and pepper. Toss salad with dressing and chill 4 hours in refrigerator before serving.

# SHRIMP COUSCOUS SALAD
### Servings: 8 | Prep: 30m | Cooks: 5m | Total: 35m

## NUTRITION FACTS

Calories: 530 | Carbohydrates: 38.7g | Fat: 28.4g | Protein: 28.7g | Cholesterol: 194mg

## INGREDIENTS

- 2 cups couscous
- salt and pepper to taste
- 2 cups water
- 1 red bell pepper, chopped
- 3/4 cup olive oil
- 1 yellow bell pepper, chopped
- 1/4 cup apple cider vinegar
- 1 1/2 pounds cooked shrimp, peeled and deveined
- 1 teaspoon Dijon mustard
- 2 medium tomatoes, chopped
- 1 teaspoon ground cumin
- 1 cup chopped fresh parsley
- 1 clove garlic, crushed

- 1 cup crumbled feta cheese

## DIRECTIONS

1. Pour water into a saucepan, and bring to a boil. Stir in couscous, cover, and remove from heat. Let stand for 5 minutes, then immediately fluff with a fork. (otherwise it will clump). Set aside to cool.
2. In a small bowl, whisk together the olive oil, cider vinegar, Dijon mustard, garlic, salt and pepper. Set aside.
3. In a large salad bowl, toss together the shrimp, cooled couscous, red and yellow bell peppers, tomatoes, parsley and feta cheese. Whisk vinaigrette to blend, then pour in about half of it over the couscous. Toss to coat, and add more dressing to coat thoroughly without drenching. Refrigerate at least 2 hours before serving.

# HONEY-MUSTARD MACARONI SALAD
### Servings: 12 | Prep: 20m | Cooks: 10m | Total: 50m

## NUTRITION FACTS

Calories: 484 | Carbohydrates: 38.1g | Fat: 33.3g | Protein: 9.5g | Cholesterol: 122mg

## INGREDIENTS

- 1 (16 ounce) package elbow macaroni
- 1 cup milk
- 6 hard-cooked eggs, diced
- 1/2 cup sweet pickle relish
- 1/2 cup diced onion
- 1/3 cup prepared honey mustard
- 1/2 cup diced celery
- 1/2 teaspoon sea salt
- 1/2 cup diced green bell pepper
- 1/4 teaspoon ground black pepper
- 2 cups mayonnaise

## DIRECTIONS

1. Bring a large pot of lightly salted water to a boil. Cook elbow macaroni in the boiling water, stirring occasionally until cooked through but firm to the bite, 8 minutes. Drain and rinse macaroni under cold water until chilled. Transfer macaroni to a large salad bowl.
2. Toss pasta with hard-cooked eggs, onion, celery, and green bell pepper. Whisk mayonnaise, milk, pickle relish, and honey mustard in a bowl and pour dressing over the salad; mix well and season with sea salt and ground black pepper.

# GREEK PASTA SALAD

**Servings: 10 | Prep: 10m | Cooks: 10m | Total: 2h20m | Additional: 2h**

## NUTRITION FACTS

Calories: 189 | Carbohydrates: 11.7g | Fat: 14.7g | Protein: 3.9g | Cholesterol: 10mg

## INGREDIENTS

- 8 ounces rotini pasta
- 3 cups sliced mushrooms
- 1/2 cup olive oil
- 15 halved cherry tomatoes
- 1/2 cup red wine vinegar
- 3/4 cup crumbled feta cheese
- 1 1/2 teaspoons garlic powder
- 1/2 cup chopped green onions
- 1 1/2 teaspoons dried basil leaves
- 1 (4 ounce) can chopped black olives
- 1 1/2 teaspoons dried oregano

## DIRECTIONS

1. Bring a large pot of lightly salted water to a boil. Add rotini pasta and cook for 8 to 10 minutes or until al dente; drain.
2. Mix together cooked pasta, olive oil, vinegar, garlic powder, basil, oregano, mushrooms, tomatoes, Feta cheese, green onions and olives. Cover and chill for at least 2 hours, serve cold.

# CHICKEN NOODLE SALAD WITH PEANUT-GINGER DRESSING

**Servings: 8 | Prep: 45m | Cooks: 10m | Total: 55m**

## NUTRITION FACTS

Calories: 461 | Carbohydrates: 51.6g | Fat: 15.8g | Protein: 30.2g | Cholesterol: 46mg

## INGREDIENTS

- 1/3 cup smooth peanut butter
- 1 (16 ounce) package uncooked linguine pasta
- 1/4 cup soy sauce
- 3 1/2 cups cooked chicken, cut into strips
- 2 tablespoons unseasoned rice vinegar

- 1 cup julienne-sliced carrot
- 1 tablespoon Asian garlic-chili sauce
- 6 green onions, chopped
- 1 tablespoon brown sugar, packed
- 1 red bell pepper, seeded and cut into strips
- 1 tablespoon finely chopped fresh ginger root
- 1 celery rib, thinly sliced
- 1/8 teaspoon red pepper flakes
- 1/2 cup fresh cilantro leaves, chopped
- 3 tablespoons low-sodium chicken broth
- 1/2 cup chopped roasted peanuts, for garnish
- salt and ground black pepper to taste

## DIRECTIONS

1. To make the dressing, place the peanut butter, soy sauce, rice vinegar, chili-garlic sauce, brown sugar, ginger, red pepper flakes, and 3 tablespoons of chicken broth together in a blender or bowl of a food processor. Blend until smooth. Season to taste with salt and pepper. Thin the dressing to your taste by adding more chicken broth or water.
2. Bring a large pot of lightly salted water to a boil. Add the linguine and cook until al dente, 8 to 10 minutes. Drain and place pasta into a large mixing bowl.
3. Add the chicken, carrots, green onions, red pepper, celery, and cilantro to the bowl with the linguine. Pour the dressing over the noodle-chicken mixture and toss until mixture is evenly coated. Divide the salad among eight serving plates, and sprinkle peanuts over each serving.

# BACON AND MACARONI SALAD
### Servings: 12 | Prep: 20m | Cooks: 15m | Total: 35m

## NUTRITION FACTS

Calories: 422 | Carbohydrates: 36.2g | Fat: 25.2g | Protein: 12.8g | Cholesterol: 96mg

## INGREDIENTS

- 1 pound sliced bacon
- 1/2 teaspoon salt
- 1 (16 ounce) package elbow macaroni
- 1/2 teaspoon ground black pepper
- 1 cup mayonnaise
- 3 tomatoes, seeded and chopped
- 1/2 cup sour cream
- 1 large cucumber, peeled and chopped
- 2 tablespoons prepared yellow mustard

- 4 hard-cooked eggs, chopped
- 1/4 cup white sugar
- 1/2 cup chopped celery
- 1/4 cup cider vinegar
- 1/2 cup sliced green olives

## DIRECTIONS

1. Place bacon in a large, deep skillet. Cook over medium high heat until evenly brown. Drain, crumble and set aside. Bring a large pot of lightly salted water to a boil. Add the macaroni pasta, and cook until al dente, 8 to 10 minutes. Drain and rinse with cold water.
2. Whisk the mayonnaise, sour cream, mustard, sugar, vinegar, salt, and pepper in a large bowl until the sugar has dissolved. Add the bacon, pasta, tomato, cucumber, egg, and celery. Gently fold until the salad is evenly covered with the dressing. Sprinkle with the sliced olives to serve.

# GRILLED CHICKEN AND PASTA SALAD
### Servings: 4 | Prep: 15m | Cooks: 30m | Total: 45m

## NUTRITION FACTS

Calories: 504 | Carbohydrates: 48g | Fat: 13.2g | Protein: 46.5g | Cholesterol: 103mg

## INGREDIENTS

- 4 skinless, boneless chicken breast halves
- 1 red onion, chopped
- steak seasoning to taste
- 1 head romaine lettuce, chopped
- 8 ounces rotini pasta
- 6 cherry tomatoes, chopped
- 8 ounces mozzarella cheese, cubed

## DIRECTIONS

1. Preheat the grill for high heat. Season both sides of chicken breast halves with steak seasoning.
2. Lightly oil the grill grate. Grill chicken 6 to 8 minutes per side, or until juices run clear. Remove from heat, cool, and cut into strips.
3. Meanwhile, place the rotini pasta in a large pot of lightly salted boiling water. Cook 8 to 10 minutes, until al dente. Drain, and rinse with cold water to cool.
4. In a large bowl, mix together the cheese, onion, lettuce, and tomatoes. Toss with the cooled chicken and pasta to serve.

# SHARESE'S SPAGHETTI SALAD

**Servings: 20 | Prep: 45m | Cooks: 15m | Total: 1h**

## NUTRITION FACTS

Calories: 239 | Carbohydrates: 21.5g | Fat: 14.4g | Protein: 6.1g | Cholesterol: 12mg

## INGREDIENTS

- 1 pound spaghetti, broken into pieces
- 1 (2 ounce) can sliced black olives, drained
- 10 slices bacon
- 2 tomatoes, chopped
- 1/2 cup chopped celery
- 1/4 cup salad seasoning mix
- 1 large onion, diced
- 1 (16 ounce) bottle Italian-style salad dressing
- 1 green bell pepper, chopped
- 1/2 cup grated Parmesan cheese

## DIRECTIONS

1. Bring a large pot of lightly salted water to a boil. Add pasta and cook for 8 to 10 minutes or until al dente; drain.
2. In a large skillet over medium heat, cook bacon until crisp. Drain and crumble.
3. In a large bowl combine spaghetti, bacon, celery, onion, bell pepper, olives, tomatoes, salad seasoning, salad dressing and Parmesan. Toss to coat. Chill until serving.

# SHANGHAI NOODLE SALAD

**Servings: 8 | Prep: 20m | Cooks: 5m | Total: 2h40m**

## NUTRITION FACTS

Calories: 258 | Carbohydrates: 41.9g | Fat: 7.4g | Protein: 5.2g | Cholesterol: 0mg

## INGREDIENTS

- 1 pound fresh thick Chinese wheat noodles
- 1/4 cup chopped green onion
- 1/4 cup ketchup
- 2 carrots, peeled and shredded
- 3 1/2 tablespoons sesame oil
- 1 small zucchini, cut into matchsticks
- 3 1/2 tablespoons soy sauce

- 1 red bell pepper, cut into matchsticks
- 2 tablespoons brown sugar
- 1 tablespoon toasted sesame seeds
- 2 teaspoons kosher salt
- 1 teaspoon crushed red pepper flakes
- 1 1/2 teaspoons lime juice

## DIRECTIONS

1. Fill a large pot with lightly salted water and bring to a rolling boil over high heat. Once the water is boiling, stir in the Chinese noodles, and return to a boil. Cook the noodles uncovered, stirring occasionally, until they have cooked through, about 5 minutes. Drain well in a colander set in the sink. Rinse the noodles with cold water several times to chill, then drain again.
2. In a large salad bowl, whisk together the ketchup, sesame oil, soy sauce, brown sugar, kosher salt, and lime juice until the brown sugar has dissolved. Place the noodles, green onion, carrots, zucchini, red pepper, sesame seeds, and red pepper flakes into the bowl, and gently toss to thoroughly mix the salad and coat with dressing. Chill at least 2 hours before serving.

# CHICKEN PASTA SALAD

### Servings: 6 | Prep: 30m | Cooks: 10m | Total: 40m

## NUTRITION FACTS

Calories: 458 | Carbohydrates: 26.6g | Fat: 33.3g | Protein: 15.8g | Cholesterol: 48mg

## INGREDIENTS

- 1/2 pound rotini/corkscrew pasta
- 1 (10 ounce) package frozen corn kernels
- 1/2 cup sliced fresh mushrooms
- 1 green bell pepper, chopped
- 1/2 cup sliced green olives
- 3/4 cup Italian-style salad dressing
- 1 stalk celery, chopped
- 1/2 cup mayonnaise
- 1/4 cup minced onion
- 1 cup canned chicken meat - drained and flaked
- 1 cup shredded Cheddar cheese
- salt and pepper to taste

## DIRECTIONS

1. Bring a large pot of lightly salted water to a boil. Add pasta and cook for 8 to 10 minutes or until al dente; drain and rinse with cool water. Pour into a large dish.

2. In a small bowl, whisk together dressing and mayonnaise; pour dressing over salad and toss again to coat.
3. Gently mix in flaked chicken; refrigerate for a few hours or serve.

# CHINESE COLD PASTA SALAD

**Servings: 4 | Prep: 10m | Cooks: 10m | Total: 1h20m | Additional: 1h**

## NUTRITION FACTS

Calories: 275 | Carbohydrates: 47.5g | Fat: 5.6g | Protein: 10.8g | Cholesterol: 0mg

## INGREDIENTS

- 8 ounces dry fettuccine pasta
- 2 teaspoons crushed red pepper flakes
- 2 tablespoons natural peanut butter
- 1 red bell pepper, chopped
- 1/2 cup vegetable broth
- 2 green onions, chopped
- 2 tablespoons soy sauce
- 1/2 cup chopped fresh cilantro
- 3 cloves garlic, minced

## DIRECTIONS

1. Cook pasta in a large pot of boiling water until al dente. Rinse and drain. Set aside.
2. In a large bowl, combine peanut butter, broth, soy sauce, garlic, and crushed red pepper. Mix well. Add pasta, sliced red pepper, scallions, and cilantro; toss to combine. Chill.

# MAGNIFICENT MACARONI SALAD

**Servings: 5 | Prep: 10m | Cooks: 10m | Total: 50m**

## NUTRITION FACTS

Calories: 783 | Carbohydrates: 53.4g | Fat: 57.4g | Protein: 14g | Cholesterol: 152mg

## INGREDIENTS

- 3 cups elbow macaroni
- 2 teaspoons rice vinegar
- 1 1/2 cups mayonnaise
- 1 teaspoon white sugar, or more to taste
- 1/3 large onion, minced

- 3/4 teaspoon celery seed
- 1/4 cup chopped fresh parsley
- 1/2 teaspoon salt
- 2 tablespoons prepared yellow mustard
- 3 hard-cooked eggs, chopped

## DIRECTIONS

1. Bring a large pot of lightly salted water to a boil. Cook elbow macaroni in the boiling water, stirring occasionally, until cooked through but firm to the bite, 8 minutes; drain.
2. Rinse macaroni in cold water until cool; drain.
3. Stir mayonnaise, onion, parsley, mustard, rice vinegar, sugar, celery seed, and salt together in a bowl; add macaroni and eggs and stir to coat.
4. Chill in refrigerate for 30 minutes before serving.

# VIETNAMESE RICE NOODLE SALAD
### Servings: 4 | Prep: 15m | Cooks: 0m | Total: 15m

## NUTRITION FACTS

Calories: 432 | Carbohydrates: 89.5g | Fat: 5.3g | Protein: 6.6g | Cholesterol: 0mg

## INGREDIENTS

- 5 cloves garlic
- 2 carrots, julienned
- 1 cup loosely packed chopped cilantro
- 1 cucumber, halved lengthwise and chopped
- 1/2 jalapeno pepper, seeded and minced
- 1/4 cup chopped fresh mint
- 3 tablespoons white sugar
- 4 leaves napa cabbage
- 1/4 cup fresh lime juice
- 1/4 cup unsalted peanuts
- 3 tablespoons vegetarian fish sauce
- 4 sprigs fresh mint
- 1 (12 ounce) package dried rice noodles

## DIRECTIONS

1. Mince the garlic with the cilantro and the hot pepper. Transfer the mixture to a bowl, add the lime juice, fish sauce or salt and sugar; stir well. Let the sauce sit for 5 minutes.
2. Bring a large pot of salted water to a boil. Add the rice noodles; boil them for 2 minutes. Drain well. Rinse the noodles with cold water until they have cooled. Let them drain again.

3. Combine the sauce, noodles, carrots, cucumber, mint and Napa cabbage in a large serving bowl. Toss well and serve the salad garnished with the peanuts and mint sprigs.

# LAP SALAD
## Servings: 10 | Prep: 20m | Cooks: 0m | Total: 20m

## NUTRITION FACTS

Calories: 185 | Carbohydrates: 6.4g | Fat: 15.5g | Protein: 6.5g | Cholesterol: 11mg

## INGREDIENTS

- 2 boneless chicken breast halves, cooked and diced
- 1 (3 ounce) package ramen noodles, crushed
- 2 ounces almonds
- 1/2 medium head cabbage, shredded
- 2 green onions, chopped
- 1/2 cup vegetable oil
- 1 tablespoon white sugar
- salt and pepper to taste
- 2 tablespoons sesame seeds
- 3 tablespoons distilled white vinegar

## DIRECTIONS

1. Combine chicken, nuts, onion, sugar, sesame seeds, noodles and their flavor packet and cabbage in large bowl. In small bowl combine oil, salt, pepper and vinegar. Pour oil mixture over noodle mixture. Let stand overnight in refrigerator and serve.

# CHARLOTTE'S TORTELLINI SALAD
## Servings: 6 | Prep: 20m | Cooks: 15m | Total: 35m

## NUTRITION FACTS

Calories: 356 | Carbohydrates: 32g | Fat: 19.5g | Protein: 15.4g | Cholesterol: 37mg

## INGREDIENTS

- 16 ounces cheese-filled tortellini
- 1 boneless chicken breast half, cooked and sliced into thin strips
- 1 green bell pepper, thinly sliced
- 1/4 cup olive oil
- 1 red bell pepper, julienned
- 2 teaspoons grated lemon zest, minced

- 1 small red onion, julienned
- 1/4 cup lemon juice
- 1/2 cup sliced black olives
- 2 tablespoons ground walnuts
- 1/2 cup crumbled feta cheese
- 1 tablespoon honey

## DIRECTIONS

1. Cook pasta in a large pot of boiling salted water until al dente. Drain and cool under cold water. Refrigerate until chilled.
2. Prepare the dressing in a small bowl by whisking together the olive oil, lemon zest, lemon juice, walnuts, and honey. Refrigerate until chilled.
3. In a salad bowl, combine pasta, peppers, red onion, olives, and chicken. Add lemon dressing and feta cheese, toss and serve.

# GREEK PASTA SALAD WITH ROASTED VEGETABLES AND FETA

**Servings: 6 | Prep: 20m | Cooks: 40m | Total: 1h**

## NUTRITION FACTS

Calories: 446 | Carbohydrates: 56.9g | Fat: 19.5g | Protein: 13.8g | Cholesterol: 17mg

## INGREDIENTS

- 1 red bell pepper, cut into 1/2 inch pieces
- 1 1/2 ounces sun-dried tomatoes, soaked in 1/2 cup boiling water
- 1 yellow bell pepper, chopped
- 1/2 cup torn arugula leaves
- 1 medium eggplant, cubed
- 1/2 cup chopped fresh basil
- 3 small yellow squash, cut in 1/4 inch slices
- 2 tablespoons balsamic vinegar
- 6 tablespoons extra virgin olive oil
- 2 tablespoons minced garlic
- 1/4 teaspoon salt
- 4 ounces crumbled feta cheese
- 1/4 teaspoon ground black pepper
- 1 (12 ounce) package farfalle pasta

## DIRECTIONS

1. Preheat oven to 450 degrees F (230 degrees C). Line a cookie sheet with foil, and spray with non-stick cooking spray.
2. In a medium bowl toss the red bell pepper, yellow bell pepper, eggplant, and squash with 2 tablespoons of the olive oil, salt, and pepper. Arrange on the prepared cookie sheet.
3. Bake vegetables 25 minutes in the preheated oven, tossing occasionally, until lightly browned.
4. In a large pot of salted boiling water, cook pasta 10 to 12 minutes, until al dente, and drain.
5. Drain the softened sun-dried tomatoes and reserve the water. In a large bowl, toss together the roasted vegetables, cooked pasta, sun-drained tomatoes, arugula, and basil. Mix in remaining olive oil, reserved water from tomatoes, balsamic vinegar, garlic, and feta cheese; toss to coat. Season with salt and pepper to taste. Serve immediately, or refrigerate until chilled.

# SPAGHETTI SALAD
**Servings: 8 | Prep: 10m | Cooks: 20m | Total: 30m**

## NUTRITION FACTS

Calories: 502 | Carbohydrates: 52g | Fat: g | Protein: 15.3g | Cholesterol: 30mg

## INGREDIENTS

- 1 pound spaghetti
- 2 tomatoes, chopped
- 1 (16 ounce) bottle Italian-style salad dressing
- 1 green bell pepper, chopped
- 1 tablespoon Italian seasoning
- 1/2 onion, chopped
- 8 ounces shredded Cheddar cheese
- 1 cucumber, peeled and chopped

## DIRECTIONS

1. Cook spaghetti in boiling salted water until al dente. Rinse in cool water, drain.
2. In a large bowl place chopped tomatoes, green bell pepper, onion and cucumber. Add Cheddar cheese, and salad seasoning.
3. Add cooled pasta to large bowl with vegetables and pour salad dressing over top. Toss well to coat. Chill for several hours before serving.

# SHRIMP AVOCADO PASTA SALAD
**Servings: 8 | Prep: 10m | Cooks: 15m | Total: 25m**

## NUTRITION FACTS

Calories: 657 | Carbohydrates: 50.4g | Fat: 38.8g | Protein: 27.6g | Cholesterol: 144mg

## INGREDIENTS

- 1 (16 ounce) package uncooked penne pasta
- 1 cup mayonnaise
- 1/4 pound bacon
- 1/4 cup lemon juice
- 1 pound cooked shrimp, peeled and deveined
- 2 tomatoes, diced
- 2 avocados - peeled, pitted and diced
- 1 teaspoon crushed red pepper
- 1 cup shredded Cheddar cheese
- 4 cups shredded lettuce

## DIRECTIONS

1. Bring a large pot of lightly salted water to a boil. Place pasta in the pot, cook for 8 to 10 minutes, until al dente, and drain. Rinse under cold running water to cool.
2. Place bacon in a skillet over medium high heat, and cook until evenly brown. Drain and crumble.
3. In a large bowl, gently toss together the pasta, bacon, shrimp, avocados, Cheddar cheese, mayonnaise, lemon juice, tomatoes, and red pepper. Serve over lettuce.

# BACON, LETTUCE, AND TOMATO MACARONI SALAD
### Servings: 12 | Prep: 20m | Cooks: 10m | Total: 2h30m | Additional: 2h

## NUTRITION FACTS

Calories: 322 | Carbohydrates: 15.5g | Fat: 25.3g | Protein: 8.6g | Cholesterol: 27mg

## INGREDIENTS

- 2 cups elbow macaroni
- 5 green onions, finely chopped
- 1 1/4 cups mayonnaise
- 1/2 cup shredded Cheddar cheese
- 5 teaspoons white vinegar
- 1/4 teaspoon salt
- 1 1/4 cups diced celery
- 1/8 teaspoon ground black pepper
- 1 large tomato, diced
- 1 (16 ounce) package bacon

## DIRECTIONS

1. Bring a large pot of lightly salted water to a boil. Cook elbow macaroni in the boiling water, stirring occasionally until cooked through but firm to the bite, 8 minutes. Drain and rinse under cold water until chilled. Transfer macaroni to a large salad bowl.
2. Stir mayonnaise, vinegar, celery, tomato, green onions, Cheddar cheese, salt, and black pepper into macaroni until thoroughly combined. Cover and chill salad at least 2 hours.
3. Place bacon in a large skillet and cook over medium-high heat, turning occasionally, until evenly browned, about 10 minutes. Drain the bacon slices on paper towels. Let bacon cool; crumble when cooled.
4. Mix bacon into macaroni salad to serve.

# KATHY'S DELICIOUS ITALIAN PASTA SALAD
### Servings: 6 | Prep: 35m | Cooks: 0m | Total: m35

## NUTRITION FACTS

Calories: 847 | Carbohydrates: 67.9g | Fat: 50.3g | Protein: 34.1g | Cholesterol: 67mg

## INGREDIENTS

- 1 (16 ounce) package dry penne pasta
- 5 roma (plum) tomatoes, chopped
- 12 ounces roasted red peppers
- 1/4 pound Genoa salami, cut into strips
- 7 ounces black olives, chopped
- 3/4 cup olive oil
- 1 small yellow onion, chopped
- 1/2 cup balsamic vinegar
- 1 clove garlic, minced
- ground black pepper to taste
- 16 ounces mozzarella cheese, cubed

## DIRECTIONS

1. Bring a large pot of lightly salted water to a boil. Add pasta and cook for 8 to 10 minutes or until al dente. Drain and rinse under cold running water until cool.
2. Mix together: red peppers, olives, onion, garlic, mozzarella cheese, tomatoes and salami.
3. Combine in large bowl, pasta and vegetable mixture. Pour in olive oil, balsamic vinegar and black pepper. Mix well together.

# ONE - TWO - THREE - MEXICAN MACARONI SALAD
### Servings: 10 | Prep: 10m | Cooks: 10m | Total: 1h20m

## NUTRITION FACTS

Calories: 368 | Carbohydrates: 39.3g | Fat: 20.4g | Protein: 7.6g | Cholesterol: 8mg

## INGREDIENTS

- 1 (16 ounce) package dry macaroni
- 1 teaspoon garlic powder
- 1 1/2 cups chunky salsa
- 1 teaspoon salt
- 1 cup mayonnaise
- ground black pepper to taste
- 1/2 cup finely chopped green bell pepper
- 1 (6 ounce) can sliced black olives, drained (optional)

## DIRECTIONS

1. Bring a large pot of lightly salted water to a boil. Add pasta and cook for 8 to 10 minutes or until al dente; rinse under cold running water, and drain.
2. In a large bowl, combine the salsa, mayonnaise, green pepper, garlic powder, salt, black pepper, and olives; mix well. Pour pasta into mixture, and stir to coat thoroughly. Cover, and refrigerate at least one hour before serving.

# ORZO AND SHRIMP SALAD WITH ASPARAGUS
### Servings: 6 | Prep: 20m | Cooks: 20m | Total: 2h40m

## NUTRITION FACTS

Calories: 302 | Carbohydrates: 33.5g | Fat: 10.8g | Protein: 18.6g | Cholesterol: 86mg

## INGREDIENTS

- 12 extra-large shrimp
- 2 green onions, chopped
- 1 clove garlic, minced
- 1 tablespoon white balsamic vinegar
- 2 tablespoons extra-virgin olive oil
- 1 tablespoon fresh lemon juice
- 2 quarts water
- 2 teaspoons honey mustard
- 8 ounces orzo pasta
- 2 tablespoons minced fresh basil
- 1 pound fresh asparagus, trimmed and cut into 1 inch pieces
- salt and pepper to taste
- 2 tablespoons extra-virgin olive oil

# DIRECTIONS

1. Peel shrimp, reserving the shells. In a skillet over medium heat, cook the garlic and shrimp in 2 tablespoons of olive oil, stirring frequently to keep the garlic from browning. When shrimp are cooked through, remove from heat, cool and cut into 1/2-inch pieces. Watch Now
2. Bring water to a boil in a Dutch oven over high heat. Add shrimp shells, boil for 5 minutes, then strain out shells and discard. Stir in the orzo and cook for 5 minutes. Stir in the asparagus pieces and continue cooking until the pasta is al dente, about 4 minutes. Drain into a mesh sieve, and rinse in cold water. Watch Now
3. Toss pasta and asparagus with 2 tablespoons of olive oil, shrimp, and green onions until evenly coated. In a separate bowl, whisk the vinegar, lemon juice, mustard, and basil until incorporated. Pour over pasta mixture and toss well; season to taste with salt and pepper. Chill for 2 hours. Watch Now.

# SALSA PASTA SALAD

## Servings: 11 | Prep: 20m | Cooks: 0m | Total: 20m

## NUTRITION FACTS

Calories: 178 | Carbohydrates: 16.3g | Fat: 12.2g | Protein: 2.7g | Cholesterol: 0mg

## INGREDIENTS

- 2 cups dry rainbow radiatore pasta
- 1/4 cup chopped fresh cilantro
- 1 onion, chopped
- 1 1/2 teaspoons garlic salt
- 1 red bell pepper, chopped
- 1/3 cup lemon juice
- 1 (6 ounce) can sliced black olives
- 1/2 cup vegetable oil
- 3 tomatoes, diced
- 1 tablespoon white sugar
- 1 (4 ounce) can diced green chiles
- 1 tablespoon chili powder
- 1/3 cup distilled white vinegar

## DIRECTIONS

1. In a large pot with boiling salted water cook radiatore pasta until al dente. Drain.
2. Meanwhile, combine chopped onion, bell pepper, olives, tomatoes, and green chilies in a large bowl.
3. In a small bowl, whisk together vinegar, cilantro, garlic salt, lemon juice, vegetable oil, sugar and chili powder.
4. Mix cooked pasta with vegetables. Toss with cilantro dressing and serve.

# ANGEL HAIR PASTA SALAD

**Servings: 6 | Prep: 15m | Cooks: 0m | Total: 15m**

## NUTRITION FACTS

Calories: 551 | Carbohydrates: 45g | Fat: 33.6g | Protein: 17g | Cholesterol: 90mg

## INGREDIENTS

- 2 (8 ounce) packages angel hair pasta
- 3/4 cup chopped green onions
- 1/2 pound cooked bay shrimp
- 1 1/2 cups ranch-style salad dressing

## DIRECTIONS

1. Cook the pasta according to package directions; drain and rinse under cold water.
2. Mix together the pasta, shrimp, green onions and ranch dressing, then carefully work the shrimp into the pasta with your hands. (Note: As the salad sits, it will absorb some of the dressing; add a little dressing right before serving).

# VEGETARIAN GREEK PASTA SALAD

**Servings: 8 | Prep: 15m | Cooks: 15m | Total: 1h**

## NUTRITION FACTS

Calories: 302 | Carbohydrates: 46.6g | Fat: 10.2g | Protein: 8.4g | Cholesterol: 0mg

## INGREDIENTS

- 1 (16 ounce) package penne pasta
- 2 tomatoes, chopped
- 1/4 cup vegetable oil
- 1 green bell pepper, chopped
- 1 teaspoon lemon juice
- 1 sweet onion, chopped
- 1 teaspoon dried basil
- 1 cucumber, coarsely chopped
- 1 teaspoon ground black pepper
- 1 cup black olives, chopped
- 1 teaspoon garlic salt

## DIRECTIONS

1. Cook pasta in a large pot of boiling water until al dente. Drain, and rinse in cold water.
2. In a small bowl, mix together oil, lemon juice, basil, garlic salt, and black pepper.
3. In a large bowl, combine pasta, tomatoes, green pepper, onion, cucumber, and black olives. Add dressing, and toss to coat. Chill in the refrigerator for 30 minutes.

# TORTELLINI PESTO SALAD
**Servings: 6 | Prep: 15m | Cooks: 8m | Total: 1h30m**

## NUTRITION FACTS

Calories: 383 | Carbohydrates: 26.1g | Fat: 27.3g | Protein: 11.2g | Cholesterol: 31mg

## INGREDIENTS

- 1 (9 ounce) package cheese tortellini
- 1/4 cup prepared basil pesto
- 1 small red bell pepper, julienned
- 1/4 cup milk
- 3/4 cup broccoli florets, blanched
- 2 tablespoons grated Parmesan cheese
- 1/3 cup shredded carrots
- 1 tablespoon olive oil
- 1/3 cup pitted green olives
- 1 tablespoon distilled white vinegar
- 1 clove garlic, chopped
- 1 bunch fresh spinach leaves
- 1/2 cup mayonnaise

## DIRECTIONS

1. Bring a large pot of lightly salted water to a boil. Place tortellini in the pot, and cook for 7 to 8 minutes, until al dente. Drain, and cool.
2. In a large bowl, mix the cooked tortellini, red bell pepper, broccoli, carrots, olives, and garlic.
3. In a separate bowl, stir together the mayonnaise, pesto, milk, Parmesan cheese, olive oil, and vinegar. Pour over the tortellini and vegetables, and gently toss to coat. Cover, and place in the refrigerator 1 hour, until chilled. Serve over spinach leaves.

# ROSEMARY CHICKEN COUSCOUS SALAD
**Servings: 6 | Prep: 35m | Cooks: 10m | Total: 45m**

## NUTRITION FACTS

Calories: 646 | Carbohydrates: 44g | Fat: 38.8g | Protein: 29.5g | Cholesterol: 68mg

## INGREDIENTS

- 2 cups chicken broth
- 2 large cooked skinless, boneless chicken breast halves, cut into bite-size pieces
- 1 (10 ounce) box couscous
- 1 cup chopped English cucumber
- 3/4 cup olive oil
- 1/2 cup chopped sun-dried tomatoes
- 1/4 cup fresh lemon juice
- 1/2 cup chopped pitted kalamata olives
- 2 tablespoons white balsamic vinegar
- 1/2 cup crumbled feta cheese
- 1/4 cup chopped fresh rosemary leaves
- 1/3 cup chopped fresh Italian parsley
- salt and ground black pepper to taste
- salt and ground black pepper to taste

## DIRECTIONS

1. Place chicken stock in a saucepan and bring to a boil over medium-high heat. Stir in couscous. Remove pan from the heat; cover, and let stand for 5 minutes. Fluff couscous with a fork. Cool for 10 minutes.
2. Meanwhile, make the dressing by combining the olive oil, lemon juice, and vinegar in the bowl of a blender or food processor; mix on low until mixture thickens. Stir in rosemary. Season to taste with salt and pepper.
3. Combine the chicken, cucumber, sun-dried tomatoes, and olives in a large bowl. Stir in the couscous, Feta cheese, and parsley. Season to taste with salt and pepper. Toss the salad with half the dressing. Taste, and add more dressing as desired, or, if making the salad in advance, add additional dressing just before serving.

# CHICKPEA MACARONI SALAD

**Servings: 6 | Prep: 10m | Cooks: 10m | Total: 50m**

## NUTRITION FACTS

Calories: 459 | Carbohydrates: 42.1g | Fat: 28g | Protein: 12g | Cholesterol: 25mg

## INGREDIENTS

- 1 cup macaroni
- 1 cup pitted black olives
- 1 (19 ounce) can chickpeas (garbanzo beans), drained
- 1 teaspoon salt

- 4 tomatoes, chopped
- 1/2 teaspoon ground black pepper
- 1 onion, chopped
- 1/2 cup olive oil
- 1 clove garlic, minced
- 1/4 cup fresh lemon juice
- 6 ounces feta cheese, crumbled

## DIRECTIONS

1. Bring a medium saucepan of lightly salted water to a boil. Add macaroni, and cook 8 to 10 minutes, or until al dente. Rinse under cold water to chill, and drain.
2. Meanwhile, combine the chickpeas, tomatoes, onion, garlic, feta cheese, olives, salt, pepper, olive oil, and lemon juice in a large bowl. Set aside to marinate while the pasta is cooking.
3. Mix macaroni with chickpea mixture. Cover, and refrigerate for at least 30 minutes to blend flavors.

# FRESH MOZZARELLA PASTA SALAD
### Servings: 4 | Prep: 15m | Cooks: 10m | Total: 25m

## NUTRITION FACTS

Calories: 370 | Carbohydrates: 42.5g | Fat: 14.4g | Protein: 16g | Cholesterol: 35mg

## INGREDIENTS

- 1 cup uncooked orzo pasta
- 1 teaspoon crushed red pepper flakes
- 1 1/2 cups cubed fresh mozzarella cheese
- salt to taste
- 2 fresh plum tomatoes, seeded and cut into bite-size pieces
- 1 tablespoon olive oil, or as needed
- 1/4 cup chopped fresh basil

## DIRECTIONS

1. Fill a large pot with lightly salted water and bring to a rolling boil over high heat. Stir in the orzo, and return to a boil. Cook the pasta uncovered, stirring occasionally, until cooked through, but still firm to the bite, about 10 minutes. Drain well, and let cool.
2. Mix the mozzarella cheese cubes, tomatoes, basil, crushed red pepper flakes, and salt with olive oil in a salad bowl. Gently mix in the orzo pasta, and toss lightly to coat the ingredients with oil.

# RAMEN NOODLE SALAD
### Servings: 12 | Prep: 15m | Cooks: 10m | Total: 25m

## NUTRITION FACTS

Calories: 249 | Carbohydrates: 23.7g | Fat: 15g | Protein: 5.3g | Cholesterol: 7mg

## INGREDIENTS

- 4 (3 ounce) packages chicken flavored ramen noodles
- 1/2 green bell pepper, diced
- 1 cup diced celery
- 4 ounces frozen green peas
- 1 (8 ounce) can water chestnuts, drained and sliced
- 1 cup mayonnaise
- 1/2 red onion, diced

## DIRECTIONS

1. Break noodles and cook as directed on package. Drain and rinse noodles under cold water.
2. In a large bowl, combine the noodles, celery, water chestnuts, red onion, bell pepper and peas.
3. Prepare the dressing by whisking together the mayonnaise and ramen noodle seasoning mix. Pour over noodle mixture and toss until well coated. Refrigerate until chilled and serve.

# QUICK ARTICHOKE PASTA SALAD
### Servings: 5 | Prep: 20m | Cooks: 4h | Total: 4h20m

## NUTRITION FACTS

Calories: 155 | Carbohydrates: 23.8g | Fat: 5.5g | Protein: 4.9g | Cholesterol: 0mg

## INGREDIENTS

- 1 cup salad macaroni, or other medium-size pasta
- 1 tablespoon chopped fresh parsley
- 1 (6.5 ounce) jar marinated artichoke hearts
- 1/2 teaspoon dried basil
- 1/2 cup mushrooms, quartered
- 1/2 tablespoon dried oregano
- 1 cup cherry tomatoes, halved
- 2 cloves garlic, minced
- 1 cup pitted black olives
- salt and pepper to taste

## DIRECTIONS

1. Bring a large pot of salted water to boil; add pasta and boil until al dente. Drain well and rinse with cold water.

2. In a large mixing bowl, combine pasta, artichoke hearts, mushrooms, tomatoes, olives, parsley, basil, oregano, garlic, salt and pepper; toss well. Refrigerate for at least 4 hours. Before serving, season the pasta dish with salt and pepper to taste.

# FUGI SALAD
**Servings: 8 | Prep: 10m | Cooks: 10m | Total: 20m**

## NUTRITION FACTS

Calories: 364 | Carbohydrates: 28.3g | Fat: 27g | Protein: 5.8g | Cholesterol: 8mg

## INGREDIENTS

- 2 tablespoons butter
- 1/2 cup vegetable oil
- 3/4 cup blanched slivered almonds
- 1/2 cup white sugar
- 1/2 cup sesame seeds
- 1/3 cup rice wine vinegar
- 1 medium head cabbage, chopped
- 1/4 teaspoon ground black pepper
- 8 green onion, chopped
- 2 teaspoons salt
- 2 (3 ounce) packages ramen noodles

## DIRECTIONS

1. In a skillet over low heat, melt the butter or margarine; add the almonds and sesame seeds. Cook until lightly toasted.
2. In a large bowl, combine the cabbage, onions, almonds, sesame seeds and broken uncooked ramen noodles.
3. Wisk together the oil, sugar, vinegar, pepper and salt. Pour over salad, toss, and serve.

# MINTY ORZO LENTIL AND FETA SALAD
**Servings: 8 | Prep: 30m | Cooks: 20m | Total: 2h50m | Additional: 2h**

## NUTRITION FACTS

Calories: 374 | Carbohydrates: 38.2g | Fat: 19g | Protein: 13.3g | Cholesterol: 25mg

## INGREDIENTS

- 1 1/4 cups orzo pasta
- 1 1/2 cups crumbled feta cheese

- 6 tablespoons olive oil, divided
- 1 small red onion, diced
- 3/4 cup dried brown lentils, rinsed and drained
- 1/2 cup finely chopped fresh mint leaves
- 1/3 cup red wine vinegar
- 1/2 cup chopped fresh dill
- 3 cloves garlic, minced
- salt and pepper to taste
- 1/2 cup kalamata olives, pitted and chopped

## DIRECTIONS

1. Bring a large pot of lightly salted water to boil. Add pasta and cook until al dente, about 8 to 10 minutes; drain. Transfer pasta into a large bowl, and mix in 1 tablespoon olive oil; cover, and refrigerate until cool.
2. Place lentils into a small saucepan, cover with water, and bring to a boil. Cover, and simmer over low heat until lentils are tender, about 15 to 20 minutes. Drain and set aside to cool.
3. Combine the remaining olive oil, vinegar, and garlic in a small bowl.
4. Remove pasta from refrigerator; add lentils, oil mixture, olives, feta cheese, red onion, mint, and dill; stir until thoroughly blended. Season to taste with salt and pepper. Cover and refrigerate for at least 2 hours.

# EASY ASIAN PASTA SALAD
### Servings: 4 | Prep: 15m | Cooks: 10m | Total: 55m

## NUTRITION FACTS

Calories: 340 | Carbohydrates: 63.9g | Fat: 4.5g | Protein: 10.7g | Cholesterol: 0mg

## INGREDIENTS

- 1 (8 ounce) package spaghetti
- 2 teaspoons sweet chili sauce
- 1 teaspoon olive oil
- 1 teaspoon sesame oil
- 6 tablespoons soy sauce
- 2 green onions, chopped
- 1/4 cup white sugar
- 1 red bell pepper, chopped (optional)
- 3 tablespoons rice vinegar
- 1 cup sugar snap peas (optional)
- 1 tablespoon toasted sesame seeds

## DIRECTIONS

1. Bring a large pot of lightly salted water to a boil. Cook spaghetti in the boiling water, stirring occasionally until cooked through but firm to the bite, 10 to 12 minutes. Drain and rinse under cold water. Transfer pasta to a serving bowl and toss with olive oil.
2. Whisk soy sauce, sugar, vinegar, sesame seeds, chili sauce, and sesame oil together in a bowl until sugar dissolves. Toss soy sauce mixture with pasta; top with green onions, red bell pepper, and snap peas. Refrigerate 30 minutes to overnight to allow flavors to blend. Toss again before serving.

# BEST MACARONI SALAD
### Servings: 8 | Prep: 15m | Cooks: 15m | Total: 4h30m

## NUTRITION FACTS

Calories: 437 | Carbohydrates: 43.8g | Fat: 23g | Protein: 13.4g | Cholesterol: 28mg

## INGREDIENTS

- 1 (16 ounce) package macaroni
- 1 cup shredded Cheddar cheese
- 1/2 cup mayonnaise
- 3 tablespoons olive oil
- 1 cup cucumber - peeled, seeded and chopped
- 3 tablespoons white wine vinegar
- 1 tablespoon dried minced onion
- salt and pepper to taste
- 1 cup diced ham

## DIRECTIONS

1. In a large pot of salted boiling water, cook pasta until al dente, rinse under cold water and drain.
2. In a large bowl, combine the pasta, mayonnaise and mix well. Stir in cucumber, onion, ham and cheese. Mix well. Drizzle oil and vinegar over top and toss. Refrigerate for at least 4 hours.

# MACARONI AND CHEESE SALAD
### Servings: 6 | Prep: 20m | Cooks: 15m | Total: 1h25m | Additional: 50m

## NUTRITION FACTS

Calories: 447 | Carbohydrates: 23g | Fat: 35.9g | Protein: 8.8g | Cholesterol: 34mg

## INGREDIENTS

- 1 1/2 cups macaroni

- 3 tablespoons thinly sliced green onion
- 2 tablespoons cider vinegar
- 8 cherry tomatoes
- 1 cup shredded Cheddar cheese
- 1 cup mayonnaise
- 1/2 cup chopped green bell pepper
- salt and pepper to taste
- 1/4 cup chopped celery
- 1/4 teaspoon Beau Monde seasoning

## DIRECTIONS

1. In a large pot of salted boiling water, cook pasta until al dente, rinse under cold water and drain.
2. In a large bowl, combine pasta and vinegar. Mix well and allow to sit 15-20 minutes.
3. Add cheese, peppers, celery, green onions, tomatoes, mayonnaise and seasonings. Mix well and refrigerate until chilled.

# COUSCOUS, CRANBERRY, AND FETA SALAD

**Servings: 2 | Prep: 10m | Cooks: 5m | Total: 15m | Additional: 5m**

## NUTRITION FACTS

Calories: 216 | Carbohydrates: 41.5g | Fat: 3.8g | Protein: 5.3g | Cholesterol: 8mg

## INGREDIENTS

- 1/3 cup couscous
- 2 tablespoons crumbled feta cheese
- 1/3 cup dried cranberries
- 2 teaspoons balsamic vinaigrette salad dressing, or to taste
- 2/3 cup boiling water
- salt to taste
- 1/2 cucumber, diced

## DIRECTIONS

1. Place the couscous and cranberries in a heatproof bowl. Pour in the boiling water, and stir with a fork. Cover the bowl with plastic wrap, and set aside 5 to 10 minutes.
2. Fluff the couscous with a fork, and fold in the cucumber and feta cheese. Season to taste with balsamic vinaigrette and salt.

# CUCUMBER AND DILL PASTA SALAD

**Servings: 6 | Prep: 10m | Cooks: 12m | Total: 30m**

## NUTRITION FACTS

Calories: 203 | Carbohydrates: 31.3g | Fat: 5.5g | Protein: 7g | Cholesterol: 16mg

## INGREDIENTS

- 2 cups macaroni
- 1 tablespoon chopped fresh dill weed
- 2 cups cucumber - peeled, seeded and chopped
- 1/2 teaspoon coarse ground black pepper
- 1 cup chopped tomatoes
- 1/2 teaspoon salt
- 1 cup low-fat sour cream
- 1 tablespoon distilled white vinegar
- 1/2 cup skim milk

## DIRECTIONS

1. Cook pasta in boiling salted water until al dente. Drain, and rinse in cold water. Transfer noodles to a large bowl.
2. In a separate bowl, mix together sour cream, milk, dill, vinegar, and salt and pepper. Set dressing aside.
3. Mix cucumbers and tomatoes into the pasta. Pour in dressing, and mix thoroughly. Cover, and refrigerate at least 1 hour and preferably overnight. Stir just before serving.

# EASY COLD PASTA SALAD
### Servings: 8 | Prep: 15m | Cooks: 15m | Total: 2h30m

## NUTRITION FACTS

Calories: 297 | Carbohydrates: 43.9g | Fat: 10.6g | Protein: 7.2g | Cholesterol: 0mg

## INGREDIENTS

- 14 ounces uncooked rotini pasta
- 10 cherry tomatoes, quartered
- 2 cucumbers, chopped
- 3/4 cup pitted black olives, sliced
- 1/2 onion, finely chopped
- 1 cup Italian-style salad dressing

## DIRECTIONS

1. Fill a large pot with lightly salted water and bring to a rolling boil over high heat. Once the water is boiling, stir in the rotini, and return to a boil. Cook uncovered, stirring occasionally, until the pasta

has cooked through, but is still firm to the bite, about 8 minutes. Drain and cool by running cold water over the pasta in a colander set in the sink.

2. Combine cooked and cooled pasta with the cucumbers, onion, tomatoes, and olives in a large bowl. Pour the Italian dressing over the salad and stir to combine. Cover and refrigerate for at least two hours before serving,

# RANCH, BACON, AND PARMESAN PASTA SALAD
### Servings: 6 | Prep: 15m | Cooks: 2h | Total: 2h45m | Additional: 2h30m

## NUTRITION FACTS

Calories: 584 | Carbohydrates: 62.8g | Fat: 28.3g | Protein: 17.7g | Cholesterol: 27mg

## INGREDIENTS

- 1 (16 ounce) package farfalle (bow tie) pasta
- 1 carrot, peeled and diced
- 1 cup prepared ranch dressing
- 1 stalk celery, diced
- 6 slices bacon
- 1 red onion, diced
- 1/2 cup shredded Parmesan cheese

## DIRECTIONS

1. Fill a large pot with lightly salted water and bring to a rolling boil over high heat. Once the water is boiling, stir in the bow tie pasta and return to a boil. Cook the pasta uncovered, stirring occasionally, until the pasta has cooked through, but is still firm to the bite, about 12 minutes. Drain well in a colander set in the sink. Transfer to a bowl, and refrigerate until cool, at least 30 minutes.

2. Meanwhile, place the bacon in a large, deep skillet, and cook over medium-high heat, turning occasionally, until evenly browned, about 10 minutes. Drain the bacon slices on a paper towel-lined plate, let cool, and chop.

3. In a large salad bowl, stir together the ranch dressing, bacon, Parmesan cheese, carrot, celery, and red onion until well combined. Lightly stir in the cooled pasta to coat with dressing, and refrigerate 2 hours to blend flavors before serving.

# SIMPLE RANCH CHICKEN MACARONI SALAD
### Servings: 4 | Prep: 20m | Cooks: 10m | Total: 30m

## NUTRITION FACTS

Calories: 393 | Carbohydrates: 26.3g | Fat: 22.4g | Protein: 20.3g | Cholesterol: 56mg

## INGREDIENTS

- 1 cup uncooked elbow macaroni
- 2 tablespoons milk
- 1 stalk celery, chopped
- 1 (10 ounce) can chicken chunks, drained
- 1 (2.25 ounce) can chopped green olives
- 1 (1 ounce) package dry Ranch-style dressing mix
- 1/4 cup mayonnaise
- 2 teaspoons paprika
- 1/4 cup sour cream

## DIRECTIONS

1. Bring a pot of water to a boil. Add the macaroni, and cook until tender, about 8 minutes. Drain, and pat dry.
2. In a medium bowl, mix together the celery, olives, mayonnaise, sour cream, milk, chicken and Ranch dressing mix. Stir in macaroni until well blended. Refrigerate for 24 hours. Stir, and sprinkle paprika over the top before serving.

# ZESTY SOUTHERN PASTA AND BEAN SALAD
### Servings: 8 | Prep: 1m | Cooks: 10m | Total: 15m

## NUTRITION FACTS

Calories: 267 | Carbohydrates: 48.6g | Fat: 4.8g | Protein: 10.9g | Cholesterol: 0mg

## INGREDIENTS

- 2 cups small seashell pasta
- 1 1/2 tablespoons ground cumin
- 1/3 cup Italian-style salad dressing
- 1/2 tablespoon chili powder
- salt to taste
- 1/2 teaspoon onion powder
- 1 (15 ounce) can pinto beans
- 1/2 teaspoon garlic powder
- 1 (15 ounce) can black beans
- 1/4 teaspoon dried red pepper flakes (optional)
- 1 (15 ounce) can whole kernel corn, drained
- salt and pepper to taste
- 3 tomatoes, chopped

## DIRECTIONS

1. Bring a large pot of lightly salted water to a boil. Add pasta and cook for 8 to 10 minutes or until al dente; drain and rinse pasta in cold water. Place in a large mixing bowl and add dressing and salt; mix well.
2. Combine pinto beans and black beans in a colander; rinse with cold water and add to pasta. Add corn, tomatoes, cumin, chili powder, onion powder, garlic powder, dried red pepper flakes and salt and pepper to taste; toss lightly.
3. Chill salad in refrigerator until ready to serve.

# FROG EYED SALAD

**Servings: 15 | Prep: 20m | Cooks: 30m | Total: 9h**

## NUTRITION FACTS

Calories: 447 | Carbohydrates: 90g | Fat: 7.2g | Protein: 5.5g | Cholesterol: 41mg

## INGREDIENTS

- 1 cup white sugar
- 2 (20 ounce) cans pineapple chunks
- 3 egg yolks
- 2 (11 ounce) cans mandarin oranges, drained
- 2 tablespoons all-purpose flour
- 3/4 cup maraschino cherries, chopped
- 2 cups pineapple juice
- 1 (16 ounce) package miniature marshmallows
- 1 tablespoon lemon juice
- 1 (12 ounce) container frozen whipped topping, thawed
- 1 (16 ounce) package acini di pepe pasta

## DIRECTIONS

1. In large saucepan over low heat, combine sugar, egg yolks, flour, pineapple juice and lemon juice. Stir and cook until thickened. Remove from heat.
2. While sauce is cooking, bring a large pot of lightly salted water to a boil. Add pasta and cook for 8 to 10 minutes or until al dente; drain and rinse with cold water.
3. In large bowl, combine cooked mixture with pasta and toss to coat thoroughly. Refrigerate 8 hours or overnight.
4. Toss pasta with pineapple, mandarin oranges, maraschino cherries, marshmallows and whipped topping. Refrigerate until serving.

# PIZZA SALAD

**Servings: 12 | Prep: 15m | Cooks: 15m | Total: 30m**

## NUTRITION FACTS

Calories: 280 | Carbohydrates: 34.2g | Fat: 11.4g | Protein: 10.1g | Cholesterol: 13mg

## INGREDIENTS

- 1 (16 ounce) package small shell pasta
- 2 cloves garlic, minced
- 1 red bell pepper, chopped
- 1 teaspoon dried oregano
- 1 green bell pepper, chopped
- 1/2 teaspoon salt
- 1 tomato, chopped
- 1/4 teaspoon ground black pepper
- 5 green onions, chopped
- 1 cup Italian-style salad dressing
- 1 (4.5 ounce) can sliced mushrooms, drained
- 1 cup shredded mozzarella cheese
- 2 1/2 ounces sliced pepperoni sausage
- 2 tablespoons grated Parmesan cheese
- 1 (2.25 ounce) can sliced black olives, drained

## DIRECTIONS

1. In a large pot of salted boiling water, cook pasta until al dente, rinse under cold water and drain.
2. In a large bowl, combine the pasta, red bell pepper, green bell pepper, tomato, green onions, mushrooms, pepperoni, olives, garlic, oregano, salt and pepper. Toss together and refrigerate until chilled.
3. Before serving, add dressing and cheese; mix together well.

# VEGAN THAI NOODLE SALAD

**Servings: 7 | Prep: 15m | Cooks: 10m | Total: 25m**

## NUTRITION FACTS

Calories: 390 | Carbohydrates: 36.9g | Fat: 22.6g | Protein: 14.7g | Cholesterol: 1mg

## INGREDIENTS

- 8 ounces Udon noodles
- 1/8 teaspoon crushed red pepper flakes
- 1/2 cup unsalted crunchy peanut butter
- 1 cucumber, julienned
- 1/2 cup milk
- 2 cups fresh bean sprouts
- 1 teaspoon grated fresh ginger

- 2 carrots, grated
- 1 clove garlic, minced
- 6 green onions, thinly sliced
- 3 tablespoons rice wine vinegar
- 1/4 cup chopped fresh mint
- 3 tablespoons soy sauce
- 1 head romaine lettuce
- 1 tablespoon dark sesame oil
- 1 cup chopped peanuts

## DIRECTIONS

1. In a large pot of lightly salted boiling water, cook the udon noodles for about five minutes or until tender. Drain and rinse the noodles under cold running water and let cool.
2. Whisk the peanut butter, milk, ginger, garlic, vinegar, soy sauce, sesame oil, and red pepper flakes in a small bowl until well blended.
3. In a large salad bowl, combine the cooked noodles, cucumber, sprouts, carrot, green onions and mint. Wisk the peanut butter dressing and pour it over the salad. Stir until well coated and serve chilled on a bed of romaine leaves. Garnish with the roasted and chopped peanuts.

# MINDY'S MACARONI SALAD
### Servings: 6 | Prep: 15m | Cooks: 10m | Total: 2h25m

## NUTRITION FACTS

Calories: 335 | Carbohydrates: 47g | Fat: 11.8g | Protein: 9.1g | Cholesterol: 116mg

## INGREDIENTS

- 2 cups dry small elbow macaroni
- 2 tablespoons prepared yellow mustard
- 3/4 cup chopped celery
- 3 tablespoons apple cider vinegar
- 1/4 cup chopped sweet onion
- 1/3 cup white sugar
- 1 (2 ounce) jar diced pimentos, drained
- 1 teaspoon salt
- 1 medium sweet gherkin pickle, diced
- 3 hard-cooked eggs, chopped
- 3/4 cup creamy salad dressing

## DIRECTIONS

1. Bring a large pot of lightly salted water to a boil. Place macaroni in the pot, and cook for 8 to 10 minutes, or until al dente. Drain and rinse under cold water.
2. In a large bowl, mix the macaroni, celery, sweet onion, pimentos, and pickle. In a separate bowl, mix the creamy salad dressing, mustard, vinegar, sugar, and salt. Stir dressing into the macaroni mixture. Fold in the eggs. Chill in the refrigerator at least 2 hours before serving.

# MOM'S SHRIMP MACARONI SALAD
### Servings: 8 | Prep: 15m | Cooks: 15m | Total: 3h30m

## NUTRITION FACTS

Calories: 221 | Carbohydrates: 14.6g | Fat: 16.8g | Protein: 3.6g | Cholesterol: 21mg

## INGREDIENTS

- 1 cup uncooked elbow macaroni
- 1 teaspoon prepared horseradish
- 1 tablespoon finely diced onion
- 1/4 teaspoon hot pepper sauce
- 1 tablespoon chopped green bell pepper
- 1 tablespoon chopped fresh parsley
- 1/2 cup diced celery
- 1/2 teaspoon celery seed
- 3/4 cup mayonnaise
- 1/8 teaspoon chili powder
- 1/4 cup sweet pickle relish
- ground black pepper to taste
- 2 tablespoons ketchup
- 2 ounces cooked salad shrimp
- 2 tablespoons white wine vinegar

## DIRECTIONS

1. Bring a large pot of salted water to a boil, add the macaroni and let it cook until al dente; drain well.
2. In a medium-size mixing bowl, combine onion, bell pepper, celery, mayonnaise, sweet pickle relish, ketchup, pickle juices, horseradish, hot pepper sauce, parsley, celery seed, chili powder, salt, black pepper and shrimp. Fold the macaroni into the mixture. Cover and chill at least 3 hours before serving.

# THE ULTIMATE PASTA SALAD
### Servings: 8 | Prep: 15m | Cooks: 10m | Total: 1h25m | Additional: 1h

## NUTRITION FACTS

Calories: 411 | Carbohydrates: 36.2g | Fat: 22.7g | Protein: 16.1g | Cholesterol: 32mg

## INGREDIENTS

- 1 (16 ounce) package uncooked tri-colored spiral pasta
- 1 (8 ounce) package mozzarella cheese, cut into cubes
- 1 head fresh broccoli, cut into bite size pieces
- 1 (6 ounce) can large pitted black olives, drained and sliced
- 1 head fresh cauliflower, chopped into bite size pieces
- 1/2 cup olive oil, or to taste
- 1 red onion, chopped
- 1/2 cup red wine vinegar, or to taste
- 2 teaspoons minced garlic
- salt and pepper to taste
- 8 ounces pepperoni slices, cut into quarters
- Italian seasoning to taste

## DIRECTIONS

1. Bring a large pot of lightly salted water to a boil. Place pasta in the pot, cook for 8 to 10 minutes, until al dente, and drain. Transfer to a bowl, cover, and chill 1 hour in the refrigerator.
2. Toss chilled pasta with the broccoli, cauliflower, red onion, garlic, pepperoni, mozzarella cheese, olives, olive oil, and red wine vinegar. Season with salt, pepper, and Italian seasoning. Chill in the refrigerator until serving.

# MACARONI AND TUNA FISH SALAD
### Servings: 8 | Prep: 10m | Cooks: 13m | Total: 23m

## NUTRITION FACTS

Calories: 301 | Carbohydrates: 44.8g | Fat: 5.7g | Protein: 16.4g | Cholesterol: 11mg

## INGREDIENTS

- 1 (16 ounce) package macaroni
- salt and ground black pepper to taste
- 2 (5 ounce) cans tuna, drained
- 1 pinch garlic powder, or to taste
- 3 tablespoons mayonnaise, or to taste
- 1 pinch dried oregano, or to taste
- 1 onion, finely chopped (optional)

## DIRECTIONS

1. Bring a large pot of lightly salted water to a boil. Add macaroni and cook for 8 to 10 minutes or until al dente; drain and cool under running water.
2. Mix both cans of tuna into the cooled pasta. Add the mayonnaise. Stir in onion, salt, pepper, garlic powder, and oregano.

# GAZPACHO PASTA SALAD

**Servings: 6 | Prep: 20m | Cooks: 10m | Total: 2h30m**

## NUTRITION FACTS

Calories: 244 | Carbohydrates: 34.4g | Fat: 10.1g | Protein: 6.3g | Cholesterol: 0mg

## INGREDIENTS

- 1/2 pound rotelle pasta
- 1/4 cup olive oil
- 4 green onions, chopped
- 1/4 teaspoon salt
- 1 cup chopped green bell pepper
- 1 clove garlic, crushed
- 1 jalapeno pepper, seeded and minced
- 1/4 cup fresh lime juice
- 2 tomatoes, chopped
- 1/4 teaspoon ground black pepper
- 1 cucumber
- 6 fluid ounces tomato juice

## DIRECTIONS

1. Bring a large pot of lightly salted water to a boil. Add pasta and cook for 8 to 10 minutes or until al dente; drain.
2. In large bowl combine pasta, onion, bell pepper, jalapeno, tomatoes, cucumber, oil, salt, garlic, lime juice, black pepper and tomato juice. Toss well and chill in refrigerator for 2 hours. Toss again before serving.

# NELL'S CABBAGE SALAD

**Servings: 6 | Prep: 10m | Cooks: 0m | Total: 10m**

## NUTRITION FACTS

Calories: 429 | Carbohydrates: 38g | Fat: 28g | Protein: 10.9g | Cholesterol: 0mg

## INGREDIENTS

- 1 medium head cabbage, shredded
- 1/2 cup olive oil
- 1 bunch green onions, chopped
- 2 tablespoons white sugar
- 2 (3 ounce) packages chicken flavored ramen noodles
- 3 tablespoons distilled white vinegar
- 4 ounces slivered almonds, toasted

## DIRECTIONS

1. In a large bowl, combine the cabbage, green onions, noodles and almonds.
2. Prepare the dressing by whisking together the oil, sugar, vinegar and seasoning packets. Pour over cabbage mixture and mix well to coat. Refrigerate until chilled and serve.

# TUNA PICCATA PASTA SALAD

**Servings: 4 | Prep: 10m | Cooks: 10m | Total: 1h20m**

## NUTRITION FACTS

Calories: 399 | Carbohydrates: 23.8g | Fat: 24.6g | Protein: 20.8g | Cholesterol: 20mg

## INGREDIENTS

- 6 ounces angel hair pasta
- salt and pepper to taste
- 1 1/2 tablespoons fresh lemon juice
- 6 tablespoons olive oil
- 3/4 teaspoon Dijon mustard
- 1 (9 ounce) can solid white tuna packed in water, drained
- 1 tablespoon mayonnaise
- 2 teaspoons capers, drained

## DIRECTIONS

1. Bring a pot of lightly salted water to boil. Add pasta, and cook until al dente, about 8 to 10 minutes. Drain, and set aside.
2. In a large bowl, whisk together lemon juice, mustard, and mayonnaise. Season with salt and pepper to taste. Slowly whisk in olive oil. Add tuna, separating into thick chunks. Add capers, and stir to combine. Pour pasta into tuna mixture, and stir gently to combine. Cover, and refrigerate.

# ORZO AND WILD RICE SALAD

**Servings: 4 | Prep: 15m | Cooks: 25m | Total: 3h**

## NUTRITION FACTS

Calories: 566 | Carbohydrates: 68.2g | Fat: 29.1g | Protein: 10.6g | Cholesterol: <1mg

## INGREDIENTS

- 1/2 cup wild rice
- 1/2 teaspoon salt
- 2 cups water
- 1/2 teaspoon ground black pepper
- 1 cup orzo pasta
- 2 tablespoons white balsamic vinegar
- 3 tablespoons chopped red onion
- 1 1/2 tablespoons honey
- 3 tablespoons dried currants
- 3/4 teaspoon Dijon mustard
- 2 tablespoons corn kernels, drained
- 1/4 teaspoon minced garlic
- 3 tablespoons diced yellow bell pepper
- 1/8 teaspoon pepper
- 3 tablespoons diced red bell pepper
- 1 1/2 teaspoons chopped fresh basil
- 3 tablespoons diced green bell pepper
- 1/4 cup canola oil
- 2 tablespoons chopped fresh basil
- 1/4 cup extra-virgin olive oil

## DIRECTIONS

1. Bring the wild rice and water to a boil in a saucepan. Reduce heat to medium-low, cover, and simmer until the rice is tender but not mushy, 20 to 45 minutes depending on the variety of wild rice. Drain off any excess liquid, fluff the rice with a fork, and cook uncovered 5 minutes more. Once finished, spread into a shallow dish, and refrigerate until cold.
2. Bring a large pot of lightly salted water to a boil. Add the orzo pasta, and cook until al dente, 7 to 8 minute. Drain, rinse with cold water, and chill.
3. Place the chilled rice and orzo into a large mixing bowl. Stir in the red onion, currants, corn, yellow bell pepper, red bell pepper, and green bell pepper. Season with 2 tablespoons basil, salt, and 1/2 teaspoon pepper. In a separate bowl, whisk together the vinegar, honey, mustard, garlic, 1/8 teaspoon pepper, and 1 1/2 teaspoons basil. Slowly whisk in the canola and olive oils until emulsified. Stir the dressing into the pasta, and refrigerate 2 hours before serving.

# TUNA, NOODLES, PICKLES AND CHEESE
**Servings: 4 | Prep: 10m | Cooks: 10m | Total: 20m**

## NUTRITION FACTS

Calories: 491 | Carbohydrates: 55.4g | Fat: 18g | Protein: 26.3g | Cholesterol: 55mg

## INGREDIENTS

- 8 ounces uncooked elbow macaroni
- 1/2 cup light mayonnaise
- 2 dill pickles, chopped
- 1/2 teaspoon prepared yellow mustard
- 6 ounces Colby-Jack cheese, cubed
- 1 teaspoon dill pickle juice
- 1 (5 ounce) can albacore tuna in water, drained and flaked

## DIRECTIONS

1. Bring a saucepan of lightly salted water to a boil. Add the macaroni, and cook until tender, about 7 minutes. Rinse under cold running water, then drain well and pat lightly with paper towels.
2. In a large bowl, stir together the macaroni, pickles, cheese, tuna, mayonnaise and mustard. Season with a splash of pickle juice, salt and pepper. Cover, and refrigerate for at least 30 minutes before serving.

# SPICY RICE NOODLE SALAD
### Servings: 6 | Prep: 20m | Cooks: 30m | Total: 50m

## NUTRITION FACTS

Calories: 278 | Carbohydrates: 28.5g | Fat: 12.5g | Protein: 13.4g | Cholesterol: 32mg

## INGREDIENTS

- 1 (6.75 ounce) package thin rice noodles
- 4 green onions, chopped
- 3 cloves garlic, minced
- 1 cup carrots, cut into thin matchsticks
- 1/3 cup seasoned rice vinegar
- ½ cup chopped fresh herbs (basil, mint, and cilantro)
- 3 tablespoons fish sauce
- 1/2 cup chopped peanuts
- 1 tablespoon Asian chili paste (sambal), or more to taste
- 1/4 cup Fresno chile peppers, cut into rings (optional)
- 1 teaspoon brown sugar
- 6 grilled boneless, skinless chicken thighs (optional)
- 1/4 teaspoon salt
- 1 teaspoon sesame oil

## DIRECTIONS

1. Place noodles in a large bowl and cover with hot water. Stir and allow to soak until softened, about 15 minutes. Drain and rinse thoroughly.
2. Combine garlic, rice vinegar, fish sauce, chile paste, brown sugar and salt in a bowl. Stir in green onions, carrots, basil, mint, and cilantro. Toss in rice noodles, peanuts, and sesame oil. Allow to sit for 30 minutes to absorb flavors. Garnish with additional green onions and peanuts. If using, top with grilled chicken and Fresno chiles.

# PASTA SALAD A LA HONEYBEAR
**Servings: 10 | Prep: 30m | Cooks: 10m | Total: 2h40m | Additional: 2h**

## NUTRITION FACTS

Calories: 358 | Carbohydrates: 38.2g | Fat: 17.1g | Protein: 13.5g | Cholesterol: 24mg

## INGREDIENTS

- 1 (16 ounce) package tri-color rotini pasta
- 1/2 cup sliced pepperoncini peppers (optional)
- 1 small red onion, diced
- 1 teaspoon Italian seasoning
- 1 cup diced roasted red peppers
- 1/4 teaspoon garlic powder, or to taste
- 1 cup cubed mozzarella cheese
- 1 pinch seasoned salt, or to taste
- 1 (6 ounce) jar marinated artichoke hearts, drained and chopped
- ground black pepper to taste
- 1/4 pound salami, diced
- 1/3 cup Italian-style salad dressing (such as Newman's Own)
- 3/4 cup sliced stuffed green olives
- 1/4 cup mayonnaise (such as Best Foods)
- 1 (4 ounce) can sliced black olives
- 1/2 cup shredded Parmesan cheese

## DIRECTIONS

1. Bring a large pot of lightly salted water to a boil; cook rotini at a boil until tender yet firm to the bite, 8 to 10 minutes. Drain and run under cold water to cool.
2. Mix rotini, red onion, roasted red peppers, mozzarella cheese, artichoke hearts, salami, green olives, black olives, pepperoncini peppers, Italian seasoning, garlic powder, seasoned salt, and black pepper in a large bowl.

3.  Whisk Italian-style dressing and mayonnaise together in a small bowl; pour over rotini mixture and toss to coat. Add Parmesan cheese and mix well. Refrigerate salad at least 2 hours before serving.

# MEXICAN FIESTA PASTA SALAD
### Servings: 16 | Prep: 20m | Cooks: 10m | Total: 2h30m

## NUTRITION FACTS

Calories: 272 | Carbohydrates: 31.6g | Fat: 14g | Protein: 6.5g | Cholesterol: 8mg

## INGREDIENTS

- 1 (16 ounce) package dried rotini pasta
- 2 green onions, sliced thin
- 1 1/2 cups medium chunky salsa
- 1 (4.25 ounce) can sliced black olives, drained
- 1 cup mayonnaise
- 1/2 teaspoon garlic powder
- 1/2 cup sour cream
- 1/2 teaspoon ground cumin, or to taste
- 1 (16 ounce) can black beans, rinsed and drained
- 1/2 teaspoon dried cilantro, or to taste
- 1 (11 ounce) can Mexican-style corn with red and green peppers, drained
- 1 teaspoon salt
- 1/2 cup chopped red bell pepper
- ground black pepper to taste

## DIRECTIONS

1.  Bring a large pot of lightly salted water to a rolling boil; cook the rotini in the boiling water until the pasta is cooked through yet firm to the bite, about 8 minutes. Drain. Rinse under cold running water until completely cooled; drain thoroughly.
2.  Whisk the salsa, mayonnaise, sour cream, black beans, Mexican-style corn, red bell pepper, green onions, black olives, garlic powder, cumin, cilantro, salt, and pepper together in a large bowl; add the cooled pasta and stir to coat evenly. Cover the bowl with plastic wrap and refrigerate 2 hours to overnight before serving.

# CHICKEN SEASHELL SALAD
### Servings: 6 | Prep: 10m | Cooks: 20m | Total: 30m

## NUTRITION FACTS

Calories: 538 | Carbohydrates: 33.7g | Fat: 36.6g | Protein: 20.4g | Cholesterol: 55mg

## INGREDIENTS

- 1 1/2 cups seashell pasta
- 3/4 cup chopped celery
- 1/4 cup cashews
- 1 (3 ounce) can mandarin oranges, drained
- 3 boneless, chicken breast halves - cooked, skinned
- 1 cup mayonnaise
- 3 ounces pineapple tidbits, juice reserved
- 1/2 teaspoon almond extract
- 2 small Gravenstein apples, peeled, cored and diced

## DIRECTIONS

1. Cook macaroni in a large pan of boiling water until al dente. Drain, and rinse. Set aside.
2. Place nuts in a dry skillet. Toast over medium heat, turning frequently, until nuts are fragrant and lightly browned.
3. In a large bowl, combine pasta, chicken, pineapple, apples, celery, mandarin oranges, and toasted nuts.
4. In a small bowl, mix together mayonnaise, reserved pineapple juice, and almond flavoring. Stir into pasta mixture, and mix well. Chill.

# MEDITERRANEAN ORZO SPINACH SALAD
### Servings: 6 | Prep: 15m | Cooks: 20m | Total: 35m

## NUTRITION FACTS

Calories: 461 | Carbohydrates: 34.5g | Fat: 25g | Protein: 25.6g | Cholesterol: 88mg

## INGREDIENTS

- 1 cup uncooked orzo pasta
- 3 tomatoes, seeded and chopped
- 2 tablespoons extra virgin olive oil, divided
- 1 lemon, zested and juiced
- 1 pound ground lamb
- 1/4 cup chopped fresh mint leaves
- 2 cloves garlic, chopped
- 1/4 cup chopped fresh parsley
- 1 tablespoon ground coriander
- 5 green onions, chopped
- salt and pepper to taste
- 1 cup crumbled feta cheese

* 4 cups fresh spinach leaves, chopped

## DIRECTIONS

1. Bring a pot of lightly salted water to a boil. Add orzo pasta, cook for 5 minutes, or until al dente. Drain.
2. Heat 1 tablespoon olive oil in a skillet over medium heat. Place the lamb and garlic in the skillet. Season lamb with coriander, salt, and pepper. Cook until evenly browned. Remove from heat, and drain.
3. In a large bowl, mix the spinach, tomatoes, lemon juice and zest, mint, parsley, green onions, and remaining olive oil. Toss with the orzo, lamb, and feta cheese to serve.

# MEXICAN ORZO SALAD

### Servings: 8 | Prep: 24m | Cooks: 10m | Total: 2h34m

## NUTRITION FACTS

Calories: 457 | Carbohydrates: 73.7g | Fat: 12.9g | Protein: 14.7g | Cholesterol: 0mg

## INGREDIENTS

* 1 (16 ounce) package orzo pasta
* 1 (15 ounce) can black beans, rinsed and drained
* 1 small red bell pepper, chopped
* 1 (8.75 ounce) can whole kernel corn, drained
* 1 small yellow bell pepper, chopped
* 1 cup chopped cilantro leaves
* 1 bunch green onions, chopped
* salt to taste
* 1 small red onion, finely chopped
* pepper to taste
* 1 (15 ounce) can chickpeas, rinsed and drained
* 5 limes, juiced
* 1 (15 ounce) can kidney beans, rinsed and drained
* 6 tablespoons canola oil

## DIRECTIONS

1. Fill a large pot with lightly salted water and bring to a boil over high heat. Stir in the orzo, and return to a boil. Cook the pasta uncovered, stirring occasionally, until the pasta has cooked through, but is still firm to the bite, about 10 minutes. Drain.
2. Place the drained orzo in a large salad bowl, and fold in the red pepper, yellow pepper, green onions, red onion, chickpeas, kidney beans, black beans, corn, cilantro, and salt and pepper to taste. Pour the lime juice and oil over the salad, toss to coat, and refrigerate at least 2 hours to chill before serving.

# PATTY'S PASTA SALAD

**Servings: 12 | Prep: 15m | Cooks: 15m | Total: 30m**

## NUTRITION FACTS

Calories: 519 | Carbohydrates: 50.9g | Fat: 27.5g | Protein: 18.6g | Cholesterol: 36mg

## INGREDIENTS

- 1 1/2 pounds seashell pasta
- 3 bunches green onions, chopped
- 1 (6 ounce) can pitted black olives, chopped
- 2 cups chopped ham
- 2 large tomatoes, chopped
- 2 cups shredded mozzarella cheese
- 4 ounces sliced pepperoni sausage, each slice cut in half
- 1 (16 ounce) bottle zesty Italian dressing
- 1/2 cup chopped green olives

## DIRECTIONS

1. In a large pot of salted boiling water, cook pasta until al dente, rinse under cold water and drain.
2. In a large bowl, combine the pasta, black olives, tomatoes, pepperoni, green olives, green onions and ham or turkey. Before serving, add shredded mozzarella and dressing. Toss well and serve.

# THREE PEPPER PASTA SALAD

**Servings: 8 | Prep: 15m | Cooks: 10m | Total: 25m**

## NUTRITION FACTS

Calories: 483 | Carbohydrates: 48g | Fat: 25.2g | Protein: 16.2g | Cholesterol: 19mg

## INGREDIENTS

- 1 (16 ounce) package tri-color pasta
- 1 red bell pepper, julienned
- 2/3 cup olive oil
- 1 yellow bell pepper, julienned
- 3 tablespoons white wine vinegar
- 1 orange bell pepper, julienned
- 1/4 cup fresh basil leaves
- 1 medium fresh tomato, chopped
- 2 tablespoons grated Parmesan cheese
- 1 (2.25 ounce) can black olives, drained

- 1 1/4 teaspoons salt
- 8 ounces mozzarella cheese, cubed
- 1/4 teaspoon ground black pepper

## DIRECTIONS

1. Bring a large pot of lightly salted water to a boil. Place pasta in the pot, cook for 8 to 10 minutes, until al dente, and drain.
2. In a blender or food processor, blend the olive oil, white wine vinegar, basil, Parmesan cheese, salt, and pepper until smooth.
3. In a large bowl, toss together the cooked pasta, dressing mixture, red bell pepper, yellow bell pepper, orange bell pepper, tomato, and olives. Top with mozzarella cheese to serve.

# SPRING SWEET PEA PASTA SALAD

**Servings: 6 | Prep: 35m | Cooks: 15m | Total: 50m**

## NUTRITION FACTS

Calories: 829 | Carbohydrates: 64.7g | Fat: 51.5g | Protein: 29.7g | Cholesterol: 84mg

## INGREDIENTS

- 1 (16 ounce) package bow tie (farfalle) pasta
- 1 pinch cayenne pepper, or to taste
- 1 tablespoon olive oil
- kosher salt to taste
- 3/4 cup sour cream
- 1/2 cup diced red onion
- 3/4 cup mayonnaise
- 8 ounces frozen green peas, thawed
- 1/4 cup lemon juice
- 8 ounces diced fully cooked lean ham
- 1 tablespoon lemon zest
- 8 ounces cubed sharp Cheddar cheese
- 1 tablespoon dried dill weed
- 2 sprigs fresh dill, for garnish

## DIRECTIONS

4. Bring a large pot of lightly salted water to a boil over high heat. Add the bow tie pasta, and cook until al dente, 8 to 10 minutes. Drain and rinse well with cold water, then toss with the olive oil, and set aside.

5. Stir the sour cream, mayonnaise, lemon juice, lemon zest, dried dill, cayenne pepper, and salt until smooth. Fold in the onion, peas, ham, Cheddar cheese, and bow tie pasta. Garnish with the dill sprigs to serve.

# NAPA CABBAGE NOODLE SALAD

**Servings: 7 | Prep: 10m | Cooks: 1h | Total: 1h10m**

## NUTRITION FACTS

Calories: 666 | Carbohydrates: 31.5g | Fat: 59.4g | Protein: 6.8g | Cholesterol: <1mg

## INGREDIENTS

- 1 large head napa cabbage, shredded
- 1 cup canola oil
- 1/2 cup olive oil
- 2 teaspoons soy sauce
- 1 (3 ounce) package ramen noodles, crushed
- 2/3 cup white sugar
- 1/2 cup sesame seeds
- 2 tablespoons balsamic vinegar
- 3 ounces blanched slivered almonds
- 6 tablespoons white wine vinegar

## DIRECTIONS

1. Place the cabbage in a large bowl, cover, and place in the refrigerator to chill for 30 minutes. Heat the olive oil in a skillet over medium heat, and cook and stir the ramen noodles, sesame seeds, almonds until lightly browned; set aside to cool.
2. Prepare the dressing by mixing the canola oil, soy sauce, sugar, balsamic and white vinegars in a blender until smooth.
3. About 30 minutes before serving, toss the dressing and cabbage mixture together; chill. Just before serving, toss the noodle mixture with the cabbage mixture.

# BACON RANCH MACARONI SALAD

**Servings: 8 | Prep: 20m | Cooks: 20m | Total: 4h40m | Additional: 4h**

## NUTRITION FACTS

Calories: 583 | Carbohydrates: 47.5g | Fat: 35.3g | Protein: 18.1g | Cholesterol: 47mg

## INGREDIENTS

- 6 slices bacon
- 1/2 small green bell pepper, diced very small

- 1 pound elbow macaroni
- 1 (1 ounce) package ranch salad dressing mix
- 1 cup mayonnaise
- 1 (8 ounce) package Cheddar cheese, cut into small cubes
- 1/2 small red onion, diced very small

## DIRECTIONS

1. Cook bacon in a large, deep skillet over medium-high heat until crisp, about 10 minutes; drain on a plate lined with paper towels until cool. Crumble the bacon.
2. Bring a large pot of lightly salted water to a boil. Cook elbow macaroni in the boiling water, stirring occasionally, until cooked through but firm to the bite, 8 minutes; drain.
3. Rinse macaroni with cold water until cool; drain.
4. Mix cooled macaroni, crumbled bacon, mayonnaise, red onion, green bell pepper, ranch salad dressing mix, and Cheddar cheese together in a large bowl.
5. Cover the bowl with plastic wrap and refrigerate at least 4 hours before serving.

# MACARONI SALAD FOR A CROWD
### Servings: 8 | Prep: 15m | Cooks: 10m | Total: 25m

## NUTRITION FACTS

Calories: 472 | Carbohydrates: 48.2g | Fat: 22.6g | Protein: 18.3g | Cholesterol: 323mg

## INGREDIENTS

- 1 (16 ounce) package uncooked macaroni
- 1 tablespoon prepared yellow mustard, or to taste
- 8 hard-cooked eggs, grated
- 1/2 cup mayonnaise, or as needed
- 1 (6 ounce) can black olives, drained and chopped
- salt and black pepper to taste
- 1 medium red onion, finely chopped
- 4 hard-cooked eggs, sliced
- 1 (10 ounce) jar dill pickle relish, partially drained
- paprika to taste

## DIRECTIONS

1. Bring a large pot of lightly salted water to a boil. Place macaroni in the pot, cook for 8 to 10 minutes, until al dente, and drain.
2. In a large bowl, toss the cooked pasta, grated eggs, olives, onion, and relish with some of the liquid. Mix in mustard and mayonnaise, increasing the amount of mayonnaise as desired. Season with salt and pepper. Top with sliced eggs, and sprinkle with paprika to serve.

# POPPY SEED CHICKEN PASTA SALAD

**Servings: 6 | Prep: 20m | Cooks: 10m | Total: 30m**

## NUTRITION FACTS

Calories: 253 | Carbohydrates: 25.3g | Fat: 12.5g | Protein: 8.5g | Cholesterol: 22mg

## INGREDIENTS

- 2 cups fusilli (spiral) pasta
- 1/4 cup chopped celery
- 1 1/2 cups cubed cooked chicken
- 1/4 cup slivered almonds
- 6 tablespoons chopped onion
- 1/2 cup poppy seed salad dressing
- 1/4 cup dried cranberries

## DIRECTIONS

1. Bring a large pot of lightly salted water to a boil. Cook pasta in the boiling water, stirring occasionally, until cooked through but firm to the bite, 12 minutes; drain, rinse in cold water, and drain again.
2. Toss pasta, chicken, onion, cranberries, celery, and almonds together in a salad bowl; drizzle with poppy seed dressing and stir to coat.

# COUSCOUS WITH A KICK

**Servings: 6 | Prep: 20m | Cooks: 10m | Total: 30m**

## NUTRITION FACTS

Calories: 210 | Carbohydrates: 38.3g | Fat: 3.3g | Protein: 8.1g | Cholesterol: 11mg

## INGREDIENTS

- 3 cups water
- 3 tablespoons chopped fresh mint
- 2 cups couscous
- 3 tablespoons chopped fresh basil
- 1/2 cup crumbled feta cheese
- 3 tablespoons chopped fresh cilantro
- 1 fresh jalapeno pepper, chopped
- 1 tablespoon chopped fresh parsley
- 1/2 cucumber, diced
- 2 teaspoons ground cumin

- 1 clove garlic, minced
- 2 teaspoons cayenne pepper
- 1/2 cup chopped green onion
- 1 lemon, juiced

## DIRECTIONS

1. Bring the water to a boil in a saucepan. Remove from the heat and stir in the couscous. Cover and let stand until the couscous absorbs the water entirely, about 10 minutes; fluff with a fork.
2. While the couscous soaks, stir the feta cheese, jalapeno pepper, cucumber, garlic, green onion, mint, basil, cilantro, parsley, cumin, cayenne pepper, and lemon juice in a large bowl. Add the prepared couscous and mix well.

# CARIBBEAN CRABMEAT SALAD
### Servings: 4 | Prep: 20m | Cooks: 10m | Total: 1h30m

## NUTRITION FACTS

Calories: 304 | Carbohydrates: 50.1g | Fat: 7.5g | Protein: 9.8g | Cholesterol: 11mg

## INGREDIENTS

- 3 cups uncooked rotini pasta
- 3 tablespoons fresh lime juice
- 1 (8 ounce) package imitation crabmeat, flaked
- 2 tablespoons olive oil
- 1 red bell pepper, julienned
- 1 tablespoon honey
- 1 mango - peeled, seeded, and cubed
- 1/2 teaspoon ground cumin
- 2 tablespoons chopped fresh cilantro
- 1/2 teaspoon ground ginger
- 1 jalapeno pepper, seeded and minced
- 1/4 teaspoon salt
- 1 teaspoon lime zest

## DIRECTIONS

1. Bring a large pot of lightly salted water to a boil. Add pasta and cook for 8 to 10 minutes or until al dente; drain and rinse under cold water.
2. Place pasta, crabmeat, red pepper, mango, cilantro and jalapeno in a large bowl and set aside.
3. In a small bowl, whisk together the lime zest, lime juice, olive oil, honey, cumin, ginger and salt. Pour over salad, toss to coat and let sit in refrigerator for at least one hour before serving.

# MAKE-AHEAD SPAGHETTI SALAD

**Servings: 8 | Prep: 10m | Cooks: 15m | Total: 13h45m**

## NUTRITION FACTS

Calories: 388 | Carbohydrates: 49.2g | Fat: 11.9g | Protein: 8.6g | Cholesterol: 0mg

## INGREDIENTS

- 1 pound spaghetti
- 1 cucumber, chopped
- 1 (8 ounce) bottle zesty Italian dressing
- 2 tomatoes, chopped
- 1 tablespoon Italian seasoning
- 1 (2 ounce) can sliced black olives
- 1 bunch green onions, chopped

## DIRECTIONS

1. In a large pot of salted boiling water cook pasta until al dente. Drain and cool under cold water.
2. Combine cooked pasta with Italian dressing, Italian salad seasoning, green onions, cucumber, tomatoes and black olives. Toss to coat and refrigerate overnight before serving.

# YUMMY COUSCOUS SALAD

**Servings: 6 | Prep: 15m | Cooks: 30m | Total: 1h45m**

## NUTRITION FACTS

Calories: 247 | Carbohydrates: 30g | Fat: 12.2g | Protein: 13g | Cholesterol: 13mg

## INGREDIENTS

- 1/2 cup creamy salad dressing
- 1 red onion, chopped
- 1/4 cup plain yogurt
- 1 red bell pepper, chopped
- 1 teaspoon ground cumin
- 1/3 cup chopped parsley
- salt and pepper to taste
- 1/3 cup raisins
- 1 tablespoon butter
- 1/3 cup toasted and sliced almonds
- 1/2 cup couscous
- 1/2 cup canned chickpeas, drained

- 1 cup water

## DIRECTIONS

1. In a medium bowl, blend creamy salad dressing, yogurt, cumin, salt and pepper. Cover, and place in the refrigerator 1 hour, or until chilled.
2. Melt butter in a medium saucepan over medium heat. Stir in couscous, and coat with butter. Stir in water, reduce heat, and a simmer, covered, until all water is absorbed, about 5-10 minutes.
3. Mix couscous, red onion, red bell pepper, parsley, raisins, almonds and chickpeas into the creamy salad dressing mixture. Cover, and chill in the refrigerator until serving.

# RAINBOW ROTINI SALAD
### Servings: 8 | Prep: 20m | Cooks: 10m | Total: 30m

## NUTRITION FACTS

Calories: 327 | Carbohydrates: 50.2g | Fat: 11.2g | Protein: 9.1g | Cholesterol: 0mg

## INGREDIENTS

- 1 (16 ounce) package colored rotini pasta
- 1 cup broccoli florets
- 2 tomatoes, chopped
- 1 cup fresh sliced mushrooms
- 1 green bell pepper, chopped
- 1 (8 ounce) bottle Italian-style salad dressing
- 1 onion, chopped
- 1 cup black olives, pitted and sliced
- 1 large cucumber, chopped

## DIRECTIONS

1. Bring 4 quarts of water to a rapid boil (2 teaspoons of salt can be added, optional). Add rotini. Return water to rapid boil and cook uncovered, stirring frequently, for about 10 to 12 minutes. Drain. Rinse in cold water.
2. Combine cooked pasta with tomatoes, green bell pepper, onion, cucumber, broccoli, mushrooms, olives and Italian salad dressing. Cover and chill. Toss salad before serving.

# CHICKEN PASTA SALAD WITH CASHEWS AND DRIED CRANBERRIES
### Servings: 6 | Prep: 35m | Cooks: 10m | Total: 2h45m | Additional: 2h

## NUTRITION FACTS

Calories: 929 | Carbohydrates: 87.9g | Fat: 50.3g | Protein: 36.6g | Cholesterol: 85mg

## INGREDIENTS

- 3 cups bow tie (farfalle) pasta
- 1 1/2 cups seedless red grapes, halved
- 1 (16 ounce) bottle bottled coleslaw dressing
- 2 (5 ounce) cans water chestnuts, drained and quartered
- 1/2 cup mayonnaise
- 2 cups thinly sliced celery
- 1/2 cup creamy salad dressing (such as Miracle Whip™)
- 1/2 cup thinly sliced green onions
- 4 cups cubed cooked chicken
- 2 cups cashew halves
- 1 1/2 cups seedless green grapes, halved
- 2 cups dried cranberries

## DIRECTIONS

1. Bring a large pot of lightly salted water to a boil. Add pasta and cook for 8 to 10 minutes or until al dente; drain, and set aside.
2. In a medium bowl, whisk together coleslaw dressing, mayonnaise, and creamy salad dressing.
3. In a large bowl, combine pasta, chicken, green grapes, red grapes, water chestnuts, celery, and green onions. Stir in dressing, and mix well. Place the salad in the refrigerator to marinate for 2 hours, or overnight. Mix in cashews and dried cranberries just before serving. Serve cold.

# BARBEQUE CHICKEN PASTA SALAD
**Servings: 12 | Prep: 30m | Cooks: 25m | Total: 1h35m | Additional: 40m**

## NUTRITION FACTS

Calories: 435 | Carbohydrates: 61.6g | Fat: 16.4g | Protein: 15g | Cholesterol: 24mg

## INGREDIENTS

- 3 skinless, boneless chicken breast halves
- 2 red bell peppers, seeded and diced
- 1 cup barbeque sauce
- 2 orange bell peppers, seeded and diced
- 1 (16 ounce) package small whole-wheat pasta shells
- 2 (15.25 ounce) cans whole kernel corn, drained
- 1 cup barbeque sauce
- 3/4 cup minced fresh cilantro

- 1 cup mayonnaise
- 2 (15 ounce) cans black beans, rinsed and drained
- 1 teaspoon ground cumin
- 2 jalapeno peppers, seeded and chopped (wear gloves) (optional)
- 1 cup jicama, peeled and diced
- 1 red onion, chopped (optional)

## DIRECTIONS

1. Place the chicken breasts into a saucepan over medium-low heat, and pour in 1 cup of barbeque sauce. Simmer the chicken until the meat is no longer pink inside, about 15 minutes. Allow to cool, and dice chicken meat.
2. Fill a large pot with lightly salted water and bring to a rolling boil over high heat. Once the water is boiling, stir in the shell pasta, and return to a boil. Cook the pasta uncovered, stirring occasionally, until the pasta has cooked through, but is still firm to the bite, about 10 minutes. Drain well in a colander set in the sink. Rinse pasta with cold water until chilled, and drain again thoroughly.
3. In a large salad bowl, whisk 1 cup of barbeque sauce with mayonnaise until thoroughly combined. Mix in the cumin, then stir in cooked chicken. Place cooked pasta, jicama, red and orange bell peppers, corn, cilantro, black beans, jalapeno peppers, and red onion into the salad bowl, and gently fold to combine with the dressing. Serve warm or chilled.

# MEDITERRANEAN CHICKEN AND ORZO SALAD IN RED PEPPER CUPS

**Servings: 4 | Prep: 20m | Cooks: 11m | Total: 1h1m | Additional: 30m**

## NUTRITION FACTS

Calories: 462 | Carbohydrates: 52.3g | Fat: 19.9g | Protein: 18g | Cholesterol: 31mg

## INGREDIENTS

- 1/2 pound uncooked orzo pasta
- 1/2 teaspoon salt
- 1/4 cup olive oil
- ¼ teaspoon ground black pepper
- 1/3 cup red wine vinegar
- 1/2 cup grape tomatoes, cut in half
- 1 teaspoon Dijon mustard
- ¼ cup black olives, cut in half lengthwise
- 3/4 teaspoon garlic powder
- 2 ounces crumbled feta cheese
- 3/4 teaspoon dried oregano
- 1 grilled chicken breast half, diced

- 3/4 teaspoon dried basil
- 2 red bell peppers, cut in half lengthwise and seeded
- 3/4 teaspoon onion powder
- 4 sprigs fresh oregano

## DIRECTIONS

1. Fill a large pot with lightly salted water and bring to a rolling boil over high heat. Once the water is boiling, stir in the orzo, and return to a boil. Cook the pasta uncovered, stirring occasionally, until the pasta has cooked through, but is still firm to the bite, about 11 minutes. Drain well in a colander set in the sink, transfer to a bowl, and let cool in the refrigerator.
2. In a small bowl, whisk together the olive oil, red wine vinegar, Dijon mustard, garlic powder, oregano, basil, onion powder, salt, and pepper. In a large bowl, stir together the cooked orzo, tomatoes, olives, feta cheese, and chicken breast meat until thoroughly combined. Pour the dressing over the orzo mixture, lightly mix to coat all ingredients with dressing, and spoon into the red pepper halves. Garnish each serving with an oregano sprig.

# CREAMY MACARONI SALAD

**Servings: 12 | Prep: 25m | Cooks: 10m | Total: 35m**

## NUTRITION FACTS

Calories: 341 | Carbohydrates: 24g | Fat: 25.3g | Protein: 5.1g | Cholesterol: 18mg

## INGREDIENTS

- 1 teaspoon salt
- 1/2 cup sour cream
- 1 teaspoon dry mustard powder
- 1 (5 ounce) can evaporated milk
- 3/4 teaspoon garlic powder
- 1/2 cup finely chopped onion
- 1/2 teaspoon paprika
- 3 tablespoons finely chopped green bell pepper
- 1/2 teaspoon onion powder
- 3 tablespoons finely chopped red bell pepper
- 1/4 teaspoon ground white pepper
- 2 tablespoons finely chopped yellow bell pepper
- 1/4 teaspoon ground black pepper
- 1/2 cup finely chopped celery
- 3 cups elbow macaroni
- 1/2 cup finely chopped carrots
- 1 1/2 cups mayonnaise

## DIRECTIONS

1. Mix salt, dry mustard, garlic powder, paprika, onion powder, white pepper, and black pepper in a small bowl.
2. Bring a large pot of lightly salted water to a boil. Cook elbow macaroni in the boiling water, stirring occasionally until cooked through but firm to the bite, 8 minutes. Drain and rinse macaroni under cold water until cooled.
3. Whisk mayonnaise, sour cream, and evaporated milk in a large salad bowl until dressing is smooth and creamy; stir in seasoning mix until well blended. Mix macaroni, onion, green, red, and yellow bell pepper, celery, and carrots into the dressing until thoroughly coated.

# SESAME CHICKEN PASTA SALAD

**Servings: 6 | Prep: 20m | Cooks: 10m | Total: 30m**

## NUTRITION FACTS

Calories: 475 | Carbohydrates: 54g | Fat: 19.4g | Protein: 23.3g | Cholesterol: 36mg

## INGREDIENTS

- 1 (12 ounce) package radiatore pasta
- 3 1/2tablespoons sugar
- 1/4 cup sesame seeds
- 2 cups cubed, cooked chicken
- 1/4 cup salad oil
- 1/2cup chopped fresh parsley
- 3/4 cup soy sauce
- 1/2cup coarsely chopped green onion
- 1/2 cup white wine vinegar
- 4 cups torn fresh spinach leaves

## DIRECTIONS

1. Bring a large pot of lightly salted water to a boil. Add pasta and cook for 8 to 10 minutes or until al dente; drain.
2. Meanwhile, heat oil in a small skillet over medium-low heat. Stir in sesame seeds and cook until golden brown. Remove from heat. Stir in soy sauce, vinegar, and sugar. Pour dressing into a sealable container, and set aside.
3. In a large bowl, mix together pasta, cooked chicken, and 1 cup dressing (reserve remaining dressing). Cover salad, and refrigerate at least 6 hours.
4. Directly before serving, stir in parsley, green onions, and spinach. Toss with remaining dressing, if desired.

# CREAMY CRAB AND PASTA SALAD

**Servings: 8 | Prep: 15m | Cooks: 12m | Total: 27m**

## NUTRITION FACTS

Calories: 295 | Carbohydrates: 35.6g | Fat: 8.6g | Protein: 19.2g | Cholesterol: 54mg

## INGREDIENTS

- 1 (12 ounce) package uncooked pasta shells
- 1/2 teaspoon salt
- 1/2 cup light sour cream
- 1/4 teaspoon ground black pepper
- 1/2 cup light mayonnaise
- 1 pound cooked crabmeat
- 1 tablespoon lemon juice
- 1/2 cup diced red bell pepper
- 1 tablespoon honey mustard
- 1/2 cup diced green bell pepper
- 1 tablespoon chopped fresh dill
- 1/2 cup chopped green onions

## DIRECTIONS

1. Bring a large pot of lightly salted water to a boil. Cook pasta shells 10 to 12 minutes, until al dente, and drain.
2. In a bowl, blend the sour cream, mayonnaise, lemon juice, honey mustard, and dill. Season with salt and pepper.
3. In a large bowl, toss together the cooked pasta, sour cream mixture, crabmeat, red bell pepper, green bell pepper, and green onions. Cover and chill until serving.

# BOW-TIE PASTA SALAD

**Servings: 6 | Prep: 20m | Cooks: 15m | Total: 3h35m**

## NUTRITION FACTS

Calories: 317 | Carbohydrates: 43.5g | Fat: 12.4g | Protein: 7.7g | Cholesterol: 15mg

## INGREDIENTS

- 1 (16 ounce) package bow-tie pasta (farfalle)
- 1/2 green bell pepper, chopped
- 1 (12 ounce) bag broccoli florets
- 2 cups creamy salad dressing (such as Miracle Whip®)

- 1 (10 ounce) basket cherry or grape tomatoes
- 1/3 cup grated Parmesan cheese
- 1 bunch green onions, sliced
- 1/4 cup white sugar
- 1/2 cup chopped celery
- 1/2 teaspoon dried basil
- 1/2 red bell pepper, chopped
- 1/2 teaspoon salt

## DIRECTIONS

1. Bring a large pot of lightly salted water to a rolling boil. Cook the bow-tie pasta at a boil until tender yet firm to the bite, about 12 minutes; drain.
2. Quickly rinse the cooked pasta in cold water to stop it from continuing to cook; drain.
3. Mix the cooled pasta, broccoli, tomatoes, sliced green onions, celery, red bell pepper, and green bell pepper in a large bowl.
4. Gently stir the salad dressing, Parmesan cheese, sugar, basil, and salt in a bowl until evenly mixed.
5. Pour the salad dressing mixture over the pasta mixture; gently toss to coat evenly.
6. Refrigerate 3 hours to overnight before serving.

# HAM AND SHELL SALAD

**Servings: 6 | Prep: 10m | Cooks: 11m | Total: 1h20m | Additional: 59m**

## NUTRITION FACTS

Calories: 365 | Carbohydrates: 33.4g | Fat: 19.6g | Protein: 16.2g | Cholesterol: 37mg

## INGREDIENTS

- 1 (8 ounce) package medium pasta shells
- 3 tablespoons mayonnaise
- 1 (10 ounce) package frozen peas, thawed
- 2 tablespoons vegetable oil
- 1/4 pound deli ham, diced
- 1 tablespoon lemon juice
- 1 cup diced Cheddar cheese
- 1/2 teaspoon salt
- 1/4 cup chopped onion
- 1/4 teaspoon pepper

## DIRECTIONS

1. Fill a pot with lightly-salted water and bring to a boil. Stir in the shell pasta and cook until the pasta is tender but firm to the bite, about 11 minutes; drain.

2. Stir the peas, ham, Cheddar cheese, onion, mayonnaise, vegetable oil, lemon juice, salt, and pepper in a large bowl; add the cooked pasta and stir to coat. Cover and refrigerate 1 hour, or until completely chilled, before serving.

# FRESH DILL PASTA SALAD
### Servings: 6 | Prep: 10m | Cooks: 10m | Total: 2h20m

## NUTRITION FACTS

Calories: 241 | Carbohydrates: 16.8g | Fat: 16.4g | Protein: 7.5g | Cholesterol: 41mg

## INGREDIENTS

- 1 (8 ounce) package seashell pasta
- 2 (4 ounce) cans small shrimp, drained
- 1 cup mayonnaise
- 1/2 cup chopped celery
- 1/4 cup sour cream
- 1/2 cup chopped seeded cucumber
- 1 1/2 tablespoons lemon juice
- 2 tomatoes, diced
- 1 1/2 tablespoons Dijon mustard
- 3 tablespoons minced shallot
- 1/4 cup chopped fresh dill weed
- salt to taste
- 1/4 teaspoon ground black pepper

## DIRECTIONS

1. Bring a large pot of lightly salted water to a boil. Add pasta and cook until tender, about 8 minutes. Drain and rinse under cold running water to cool.
2. In a serving bowl, combine the mayonnaise, sour cream, lemon juice, mustard, dill and black pepper. Gently stir in the pasta, shrimp, celery, cucumber, tomato and shallots. Mix in salt to taste and refrigerate for at least 2 hours before serving.

# GRANDMA BELLOWS' LEMONY SHRIMP MACARONI SALAD WITH HERBS
### Servings: 12 | Prep: 30m | Cooks: 15m | Total: 1h45m

## NUTRITION FACTS

Calories: 214 | Carbohydrates: 9g | Fat: 16.4g | Protein: 8.1g | Cholesterol: 90mg

## INGREDIENTS

- 3 eggs
- 1 tablespoon coarsely chopped fresh parsley
- 1 cup uncooked ditalini pasta
- 1/4 cup fresh lemon juice
- 2 (4.5 ounce) cans small shrimp, drained and chopped, or more to taste
- 1 cup mayonnaise
- 3 stalks celery, finely chopped
- salt and pepper to taste
- 2 green onions, finely sliced
- 1 sprig fresh dill for garnish, or as needed
- 1/2 teaspoon finely chopped fresh dill
- 1 sprig fresh parsley for garnish, or as needed

## DIRECTIONS

1. Place the eggs into a saucepan in a single layer and fill with water to cover the eggs by 1 inch. Cover the saucepan and bring the water to a boil; remove from heat and let the eggs stand in the hot water for 15 minutes. Drain the hot water; cool the eggs under cold running water in the sink. Peel and set aside.
2. While the eggs are cooking, fill a large pot with lightly salted water and bring to a rolling boil. Stir in the ditalini pasta, and return to a boil. Cook uncovered, stirring occasionally, until the pasta has cooked through, but is still firm to the bite, about 8 minutes. Drain. Rinse the pasta in cold water until cool and drain thoroughly.
3. In a large salad bowl, lightly toss the cooked ditalini, shrimp, celery, green onions, chopped dill, chopped parsley, lemon juice, and mayonnaise until thoroughly combined. Season with salt and pepper. Slice the hard-cooked eggs, and retain several pretty slices for garnish. Gently fold in the rest of the eggs. Arrange reserved egg slices, sprigs of dill, and parsley sprigs on top of the salad; chill for 1 to 2 hours before serving.

# THAI RICE NOODLE SALAD

### Servings: 4 | Prep: 20m | Cooks: 10m | Total: 30m

## NUTRITION FACTS

Calories: 472 | Carbohydrates: 65.2g | Fat: 21.9g | Protein: 3.9g | Cholesterol: 0mg

## INGREDIENTS

- 1 (8 ounce) package dried rice noodles
- 2 cloves garlic, minced
- 1 tablespoon olive oil
- 1/3 cup olive oil
- 1/4 head romaine lettuce, chopped

- 1/4 cup rice vinegar
- 1/4 red bell pepper, diced
- 1/4 cup soy sauce
- 1/4 cup chopped red onion
- 1/4 cup white sugar
- 3 green onions, chopped
- 1 lemon, juiced
- 1/4 cucumber, diced
- 1 lime, juiced
- 2 tablespoons chopped fresh basil, or to taste
- 1 teaspoon salt
- 2 tablespoons chopped fresh cilantro, or to taste
- 1/4 teaspoon ground turmeric
- 1 (1 inch) piece fresh ginger root, minced
- 1/4 teaspoon paprika
- 1/4 jalapeno pepper, seeded and minced

## DIRECTIONS

1. Fill a bowl with boiling water; add rice noodles. Cover bowl and let sit until noodles are softened, about 10 minutes. Drain. Add 1 tablespoon olive oil and toss to coat.
2. Mix romaine lettuce, red bell pepper, red onion, green onions, cucumber, basil, cilantro, ginger root, jalapeno pepper, and garlic with rice noodles.
3. Whisk 1/3 cup olive oil, rice vinegar, soy sauce, white sugar, lemon juice, lime juice, salt, turmeric, and paprika together in a bowl; pour over rice noodle mixture and toss to coat.

# MACARONI SALAD WITH A TWIST
### Servings: 8 | Prep: 20m | Cooks: 8m | Total: 4h28m

## NUTRITION FACTS

Calories: 582 | Carbohydrates: 64.1g | Fat: 29.2g | Protein: 17.7g | Cholesterol: 44mg

## INGREDIENTS

- 1 (16 ounce) package small seashell pasta
- 1/2 teaspoon ground black pepper
- 1 cup mayonnaise
- 1 large Vidalia or sweet onion, chopped
- 1/4 cup distilled white vinegar
- 2 stalks celery, chopped
- 2/3 cup white sugar
- 1 green bell pepper, seeded and chopped

- 2 1/2 tablespoons prepared yellow mustard
- 1/4 cup grated carrots
- 1 1/2 teaspoons salt
- 1 pound diced cooked ham

## DIRECTIONS

1. Bring a large pot of lightly salted water to a boil. Add pasta, and cook until al dente, 8 to 10 minutes. Drain pasta, but do not rinse. Let stand 5 minutes.
2. To make the dressing, combine the mayonnaise, vinegar, sugar, mustard, salt, and pepper in a bowl. Set aside.
3. Combine the onion, celery, bell pepper, carrots, and ham in a large bowl. Stir in the dressing. Add the pasta and toss gently to blend all ingredients. Chill at least 4 hours before serving.

# FABULOUS PESTO PASTA SALAD
### Servings: 8 | Prep: 15m | Cooks: 15m | Total: 1h30m

## NUTRITION FACTS

Calories: 505 | Carbohydrates: 50.7g | Fat: 26.7g | Protein: 18.9g | Cholesterol: 20mg

## INGREDIENTS

- 1 1/2 tablespoons white sugar
- 1/3 cup red wine vinegar
- 1 teaspoon salt, or to taste
- 1/2 cup olive oil
- 1 1/2 teaspoons ground black pepper
- 1 teaspoon lemon juice
- 1 teaspoon onion powder
- 1 (4 ounce) package grated Parmesan cheese
- 1 1/2 teaspoons Dijon mustard
- 4 roma (plum) tomatoes, chopped
- 2 cloves garlic, chopped
- 6 green onions, chopped
- 1 1/2 cups chopped fresh basil
- 1 (4 ounce) can minced black olives
- 1/2 cup chopped fresh oregano
- 1 (16 ounce) package farfalle (bow tie) pasta
- 1/4 cup chopped fresh cilantro
- 1/2 cup pine nuts
- 2 teaspoons hot pepper sauce (e.g. Tabasco)
- 1 cup shredded mozzarella cheese

# DIRECTIONS

1. In a large bowl, whisk together the sugar, salt, pepper, onion powder, mustard, garlic, basil, oregano, cilantro, hot pepper sauce, red wine vinegar, olive oil, lemon juice, and Parmesan cheese. Add the tomatoes, green onions and olives to the bowl, and stir to coat. Refrigerate.
2. Bring a large pot of lightly salted water to a boil. Add the pasta, and cook for 7 minutes, or until tender. Drain, and rinse with cold water to cool. Add pasta to the bowl of dressing, and mix well. Top with mozzarella cheese and pine nuts. Refrigerate for at least 1 hour before serving.

# CAPRESE PASTA SALAD

**Servings: 8 | Prep: 25m | Cooks: 15m | Total: 1h25m**

## NUTRITION FACTS

Calories: 354 | Carbohydrates: 44g | Fat: 14.6g | Protein: 13.2g | Cholesterol: 15mg

## INGREDIENTS

- 1 (16 ounce) package fusilli pasta
- 1/4 cup olive oil
- 1 cup fresh basil leaves
- 1 pint cherry tomatoes, halved
- 1/4 cup grated Parmesan or Romano cheese
- 3 tablespoons grated Parmesan cheese
- 1/4 cup pine nuts, toasted (optional)
- 4 ounces fresh mozzarella cheese, cut into strips
- 2 cloves garlic
- salt and pepper to taste

## DIRECTIONS

1. Fill a large pot with lightly salted water and bring to a rolling boil over high heat. Once the water is boiling, stir in the fusilli, and return to a boil. Cook the pasta uncovered, stirring occasionally, until the pasta has cooked through, but is still firm to the bite, about 12 minutes. Drain.
2. Place basil, 1/4 cup Parmesan cheese, pine nuts, and garlic into a blender or food processor; cover and chop to a coarse paste. Add the olive oil in a slow, steady stream. Continue processing until a soft paste has formed. Set pesto aside.
3. Combine the cooked pasta, tomatoes, 3 tablespoons Parmesan, mozzarella, and pesto in a large bowl. Season with salt and pepper. Cover bowl, refrigerate to chill for 45 minutes, and serve.

# HAWAIIAN BRUDDAH POTATO MAC (MACARONI) SALAD

**Servings: 20 | Prep: 30m | Cooks: 20m | Total: 8h50m**

Calories: 387 | Carbohydrates: 30.2g | Fat: 27.7g | Protein: 5.7g | Cholesterol: 59mg

## INGREDIENTS

- 5 eggs
- 1 teaspoon celery seed
- 7 large potatoes, peeled and cubed
- salt and black pepper to taste
- 1 cup elbow macaroni
- 2 cups grated carrots
- 3 cups mayonnaise
- 1 cup frozen green peas, cooked, drained
- 1 tablespoon sherry vinegar (optional)
- 1 small sweet onion, finely chopped
- 1 1/2 teaspoons curry powder

## DIRECTIONS

1. Place the eggs into a saucepan in a single layer and fill with water to cover the eggs by 1 inch. Cover the saucepan and bring the water to a boil over high heat. Once the water is boiling, remove from the heat and let the eggs stand in the hot water for 15 minutes. Pour out the hot water, then cool the eggs under cold running water in the sink; peel and chop the cooled eggs.
2. Bring a large pot of salted water to a boil. Add potatoes and cook until tender but still firm, about 15 minutes. Drain and set in the refrigerator to cool.
3. Fill a large pot with lightly salted water and bring to a rolling boil over high heat. Once the water is boiling, stir in the macaroni, and return to a boil. Cook the pasta uncovered, stirring occasionally, until the pasta has cooked through, but is still firm to the bite, about 8 minutes. Drain in a colander set in the sink; rinse with cold water.
4. Whisk together the mayonnaise, vinegar, curry powder, celery seed, salt, and pepper in a bowl. Combine the cooled potatoes, macaroni, chopped eggs, carrots, peas, and onion in a large bowl. Carefully stir in the dressing; cover and refrigerate overnight.

# EAGLE SALAD

**Servings: 5 | Prep: 10m | Cooks: 10m | Total: 20m**

## NUTRITION FACTS

Calories: 222 | Carbohydrates: 34.1g | Fat: 3.8g | Protein: 12.1g | Cholesterol: 10mg

## INGREDIENTS

- 2 cups elbow macaroni
- 1 (5 ounce) can tuna, drained
- 3 tablespoons mayonnaise

- salt and ground black pepper to taste
- 1/2 small onion, chopped

## DIRECTIONS

1. Bring a pot of lightly salted water to a boil. Add macaroni, and cook until al dente, about 8 minutes. Drain, and rinse with cold water to chill. Set aside to dry.
2. Mix together the cooled macaroni noodles, mayonnaise, onion and tuna in a bowl. Taste and add more mayonnaise, if desired. Season with salt and black pepper. Refrigerate until serving.

# ASIAN NOODLE SALAD
**Servings: 4 | Prep: 15m | Cooks: 8m | Total: 23m**

## NUTRITION FACTS

Calories: 230 | Carbohydrates: 36.6g | Fat: 4.8g | Protein: 8.7g | Cholesterol: 41mg

## INGREDIENTS

- 8 ounces capellini pasta
- 3 tablespoons soy sauce
- 1/2 pound shiitake mushrooms
- 1 tablespoon vegetable oil
- 1 red bell pepper, thinly sliced
- 1 teaspoon grated fresh ginger
- 1/4 cup rice vinegar
- 1 tablespoon chopped fresh parsley

## DIRECTIONS

1. Cook pasta in a large pot of boiling water. Meanwhile, clean, stem, and slice mushrooms. Add mushrooms and red bell pepper during last 2 minutes of cooking. Drain.
2. In a small bowl, mix together vinegar, soy sauce, oil, and ginger.
3. Transfer pasta, mushrooms, and pepper to a serving bowl; toss with ginger dressing. Sprinkle with parsley before serving.

# ITALIAN PASTA VEGGIE SALAD
**Servings: 8 | Prep: 10m | Cooks: 15m | Total: 25m**

## NUTRITION FACTS

Calories: 181 | Carbohydrates: 38.1g | Fat: 0.7g | Protein: 5.4g | Cholesterol: 0mg

## INGREDIENTS

- 10 ounces fusilli pasta
- 2 tomatoes, chopped
- 1 onion, chopped
- 1 cup chopped mushrooms
- 1 green bell pepper, chopped
- 3/4 cup fat free Italian-style dressing

## DIRECTIONS

1. In a large pot of salted boiling water, cook pasta until al dente, rinse under cold water and drain.
2. In a large bowl, combine the pasta, onion, bell pepper, tomatoes and mushrooms. Pour enough dressing over to coat; toss and refrigerate until chilled.

# JUSTIN'S MACARONI SALAD

**Servings: 10 | Prep: 20m | Cooks: 10m | Total: 30m**

## NUTRITION FACTS

Calories: 276 | Carbohydrates: 40.3g | Fat: 9.4g | Protein: 6.9g | Cholesterol: 8mg

## INGREDIENTS

- 1 (16 ounce) package elbow macaroni
- 1 (6 ounce) can pitted black olives, chopped
- 1 cup creamy salad dressing
- 1/2 cup chopped Vidalia onion
- 1 tablespoon cider vinegar
- 1/2 cup chopped green bell pepper
- 2 tablespoons milk
- salt and ground black pepper to taste
- 1 1/2 stalks celery, chopped

## DIRECTIONS

1. Bring a large pot of lightly salted water to a boil. Add macaroni, and cook for 8 to 10 minutes or until al dente; drain.
2. In a medium bowl, blend creamy salad dressing, cider vinegar, and milk.
3. In a large bowl, mix the cooked macaroni, celery, olives, Vidalia onion, and green bell pepper. Toss with the creamy salad dressing mixture. Season with salt and pepper. Cover and chill until serving.

# COUSCOUS FETA SALAD

**Servings: 8 | Prep: 15m | Cooks: 5m | Total: 2h | Additional: 1h40m**

## NUTRITION FACTS

Calories: 304 | Carbohydrates: 26.8g | Fat: 18.9g | Protein: 7.3g | Cholesterol: 13mg

## INGREDIENTS

- 2 cups water
- 1/2 cup olive oil
- 1 1/3 cups couscous
- 1 cucumber, seeded and chopped
- 1 teaspoon salt
- 1 (4 ounce) container crumbled feta cheese
- 1/2 teaspoon ground black pepper
- 6 green onions, chopped
- 2 tablespoons red wine vinegar
- 1/2 cup chopped fresh parsley
- 1 1/2 tablespoons Dijon mustard
- 1/4 cup toasted pine nuts

## DIRECTIONS

1. Bring the water to a boil in a saucepan over high heat. Remove from the heat, and stir in the couscous. Cover, and let stand for 10 minutes. Scrape the couscous into a mixing bowl, fluff with a fork, and refrigerate until cold, about 1 hour.
2. Once the couscous is cold, make the dressing by whisking together the salt, black pepper, red wine vinegar, and Dijon mustard in a small bowl. Slowly drizzle in the olive oil while continuing to whisk until the oil has thickened the dressing. Fold the cucumber, feta cheese, green onions, parsley, and pine nuts into the couscous. Pour the dressing overtop, and stir until evenly moistened. Chill 30 minutes before serving.

# HEALTHIER CLASSIC MACARONI SALAD
### Servings: 10 | Prep: 20m | Cooks: 10m | Total: 4h30m

## NUTRITION FACTS

Calories: 281 | Carbohydrates: 28.1g | Fat: 18g | Protein: 4.2g | Cholesterol: 8mg

## INGREDIENTS

- 4 cups whole wheat elbow macaroni
- 1 large onion, chopped
- 1 cup mayonnaise
- 2 stalks celery, chopped
- 1/4 cup distilled white vinegar
- 1 green bell pepper, seeded and chopped
- 1/3 cup white sugar

- 1 red bell pepper, seeded and chopped
- 2 1/2 tablespoons prepared yellow mustard
- 1/4 cup grated carrot
- 1 1/2 teaspoons salt
- 2 tablespoons chopped pimento peppers (optional)
- 1/2 teaspoon ground black pepper

## DIRECTIONS

1. Bring a large pot of lightly salted water to a boil. Cook elbow macaroni in boiling water, stirring occasionally until cooked through but firm to the bite, about 8 minutes. Rinse under cold water and drain.
2. Mix mayonnaise, vinegar, sugar, mustard, salt, and pepper together in a large bowl. Stir in onion, celery, green bell pepper, red bell pepper, carrot, pimentos, and macaroni. Refrigerate for at least 4 hours or overnight, before serving.

# CLASSIC ITALIAN PASTA SALAD

**Servings: 8 | Prep: 20m | Cooks: 0m | Total: 20m**

## NUTRITION FACTS

Calories: 233 | Carbohydrates: 26.2g | Fat: 12.2g | Protein: 6.6g | Cholesterol: 9mg

## INGREDIENTS

- 8 ounces rotelle or spiral pasta, cooked and drained
- 1/3 cup sliced pitted ripe olives (optional)
- 2 1/2 cups assorted cut-up vegetables (broccoli, carrots, tomatoes, bell peppers, cauliflower, onions and mushrooms)
- 1 cup Wish-Bone Italian Dressing
- 1/2 cup cubed Cheddar or mozzarella cheese

## DIRECTIONS

1. Combine all ingredients except Wish-Bone(R) Italian Dressing in large bowl. Add Dressing; toss well. Serve chilled or at room temperature.

# PASTA CHICKPEA SALAD

**Servings: 6 | Prep: 15m | Cooks: 35m | Total: 14h**

## NUTRITION FACTS

Calories: 424 | Carbohydrates: 68.9g | Fat: 10.3g | Protein: 15.6g | Cholesterol: 6mg

## INGREDIENTS

- 1 (16 ounce) package rotelle pasta
- 1 bunch green onions, chopped
- 2 tablespoons extra virgin olive oil
- 1 (15 ounce) can garbanzo beans (chickpeas), drained and rinsed
- 1/2 cup chopped oil-cured olives
- 1/4 cup red wine vinegar
- 2 tablespoons minced fresh oregano
- 1/2 cup grated Parmesan cheese
- 2 tablespoons chopped fresh parsley
- salt and pepper to taste

## DIRECTIONS

1. Bring a large pot of salted water to a boil, add pasta and cook until al dente. Drain and rinse under cold water. Set aside to chill.
2. In a large skillet heat the olive oil over medium low heat. Add the olives, oregano, parsley, scallions and chickpeas. Cook over low for about 20 minutes. Set aside to cool.
3. In a large bowl toss the pasta with the chickpea mixture. Ad the vinegar, grated cheese and salt and pepper to taste. Let sit in refrigerator overnight. When ready to serve taste for seasoning and add more vinegar, olive oil and salt and pepper if desired.

# KIM'S SUMMER CUCUMBER PASTA SALAD
### Servings: 8 | Prep: 15m | Cooks: 15m | Total: 2h30m

## NUTRITION FACTS

Calories: 227 | Carbohydrates: 48.7g | Fat: 2.5g | Protein: 4.3g | Cholesterol: 0mg

## INGREDIENTS

- 1 (8 ounce) package bow tie pasta
- 1 cup water
- 1 large cucumber, thinly sliced
- 1 tablespoon vegetable oil
- 1 large onion, thinly sliced
- 1 tablespoon prepared mustard
- 1 1/2 teaspoons dried dill
- 1/2 teaspoon salt
- 3/4 cup white vinegar
- 1/2 teaspoon ground black pepper
- 1 cup white sugar

## DIRECTIONS

1. Bring a large pot of lightly salted water to a boil. Cook the bow tie pasta at a boil, stirring occasionally, until cooked through yet firm to the bite, about 12 minutes. Drain and rinse several times with cold water until pasta is cool.
2. Stir pasta, cucumber, onion, and dill in a salad bowl. Whisk vinegar, sugar, water, vegetable oil, mustard, salt, and black pepper in a separate bowl until sugar and salt have dissolved. Pour dressing over the pasta mixture and toss lightly to coat with dressing. Let chill for 2 hours before serving.

# SOBA NOODLE SALAD WITH CHICKEN AND SESAME
### Servings: 3 | Prep: 20m | Cooks: 7m | Total: 27m

## NUTRITION FACTS

Calories: 339 | Carbohydrates: 38.3g | Fat: 15.2g | Protein: 15.5g | Cholesterol: 23mg

## INGREDIENTS

- 2 tablespoons rice vinegar
- 1 teaspoon chopped garlic
- 1 tablespoon vegetable oil
- salt and ground black pepper to taste
- 1 tablespoon sesame oil
- 1 rib celery, sliced (optional)
- 1 tablespoon brown sugar
- 1 carrot, sliced
- 1 tablespoon soy sauce
- 1/2 red bell pepper, chopped
- 2 teaspoons minced fresh ginger root
- 1/4 cup chopped fresh cilantro
- 4 ounces buckwheat soba noodles
- 2 tablespoons chopped green onion
- 2 teaspoons vegetable oil
- 1 tablespoon sesame seeds
- 1 boneless skinless chicken breast, cut into thin bite-size strips

## DIRECTIONS

1. Whisk rice vinegar, 1 tablespoon vegetable oil, sesame oil, brown sugar, soy sauce, and ginger together in a large bowl until dressing is combined.
2. Bring water to a boil in a large pot. Add soba noodles, stir, and return water to a boil. Boil noodles until tender, 4 to 5 minutes. Drain noodles in a colander under cold running water until cool, about 1 minut

3. Heat 2 teaspoons vegetable oil in a skillet over medium heat. Cook chicken breast pieces until no longer pink in the center and the juices run clear, 2 to 4 minutes. Add garlic, salt, and pepper; stir until fragrant, about 1 minute more.
4. Toss soba noodles, chicken, celery, carrot, red pepper, cilantro, green onion, and sesame seeds together with dressing in large bowl.

# ASIAN BEEF NOODLE SALAD

**Servings: 7 | Prep: 30m | Cooks: 10m | Total: 40m**

## NUTRITION FACTS

Calories: 209 | Carbohydrates: 17.2g | Fat: 9.9g | Protein: 19.9g | Cholesterol: 39mg

## INGREDIENTS

- 1 pound ground beef
- 2 tablespoons red wine vinegar
- 3/4 cup seashell pasta
- 1 tablespoon honey
- 4 cups shredded napa cabbage
- 1 tablespoon lemon juice
- 1 1/2 cups shredded carrots
- 1 tablespoon olive oil
- 1 cup sliced green onions
- 1/2 teaspoon red pepper flakes
- 2 tablespoons soy sauce

## DIRECTIONS

1. Heat a large skillet over medium-high heat. Cook and stir beef in the hot skillet until browned and crumbly, 5 to 7 minutes; drain and discard grease.
2. Bring a pot of lightly salted water to a boil. Cook shell pasta in the boiling water, stirring occasionally until cooked through but firm to the bite, 8 minutes. Drain.
3. Mix ground beef, Napa cabbage, carrots, and green onions in a large salad bowl; stir in cooked shell pasta.
4. Whisk soy sauce, red wine vinegar, honey, lemon juice, olive oil, and red pepper flakes together in a small bowl; drizzle over salad and stir thoroughly to coat.

# DELICIOUS SALMON PASTA SALAD

**Servings: 5 | Prep: 25m | Cooks: 10m | Total: 35m**

## NUTRITION FACTS

Calories: 695 | Carbohydrates: 44.9g | Fat: 48.9g | Protein: 23.1g | Cholesterol: 25mg

## INGREDIENTS

- 1 (8 ounce) package farfalle pasta
- 3 tablespoons red wine vinegar
- 2 heads broccoli, separated into florets
- 2 cloves garlic, pressed
- 2 carrots, peeled and chopped
- 3 tablespoons fresh lemon juice
- 1 cup olive oil
- salt and pepper to taste
- 2 teaspoons soy sauce
- 10 ounces canned salmon, drained

## DIRECTIONS

1. Bring a large pot of lightly salted water to a boil. Add pasta and cook until al dente, 8 to 10 minutes; drain.
2. Bring a separate large pot of water to a boil. Add the broccoli and carrots, and cook in the boiling water until tender, 2 to 3 minutes; drain.
3. Combine the olive oil, soy sauce, red wine vinegar, garlic, lemon juice, salt, and pepper in a sealable container; seal. Shake vigorously to make the dressing.
4. Toss together the drained pasta, drained vegetables, salmon, and dressing in a large bowl. Store in refrigerator up to 4 days.

Made in the USA
Las Vegas, NV
06 October 2024

96364640R00063